Free Children and Democratic Schools

Free Children and Democratic Schools:

A Philosophical Study of Liberty and Education

Rosemary Chamberlin

The Falmer Press

(A member of the Taylor & Francis Group)
New York • Philadelphia • London

UK   The Falmer Press, Falmer House, Barcombe, Lewes, East Sussex, BN8 5DL

USA   The Falmer Press, Taylor & Francis Inc., 242 Cherry Street, Philadelphia, PA 19106-1906

First published 1989

British Library Cataloguing in Publication Data
Chamberlin, Rosemary
   Free children and democratic schools:
   a philosophical study of liberty and education.
   1. Great Britain. Schools. Students.
   Personal freedom
   I. Title
   ISBN 1-85000-579-6
   ISBN 1-85000-580-X (pbk.)

Typeset in 12/14 Bembo by
Chapterhouse Typesetting Ltd, Formby, Lancs

Jacket design by Caroline Archer

Printed in Great Britain by Taylor & Francis (Printers) Ltd, Basingstoke

Contents

Acknowledgments

To Gordon who read it; to Jane and David who survived it; and to the children of Bank Leaze Infant School who never let me forget what it's really like.

Chapter 1

Introduction

'I think you've chosen the wrong time to write about freedom and education' I was told, and although obviously I disagreed it was a reasonable enough comment. There is talk of freedom in the air, on the air and in the newspapers all the time, but while the freedoms to buy whatever you can afford, and sell what you like to whomever you can are highly prized, other freedoms are less so. The freedom, imagined or real, that was supposedly given to the children of the sixties is now blamed for many of our social ills; while the freedom of teachers to plan the curriculum, and of children to select their courses is said to have caused our economic ills. In our present political climate freedom and education are spoken of in the same breath, but this is usually in the context of freedom for parents to choose their children's school, or the freedom of schools to opt out of Local Authority control. Freedom for children is not on the agenda. I think it is time we reassessed and clarified our views on liberty, and thought what they should mean for children in school.

The views about freedom which a society holds have important implications for the way children are brought up and educated. In our society, however, the relationship between what is claimed about the value of liberty and what actually goes on in our schools, homes and communities is less close than it might be, and this is due, I suggest, to the exclusion of children from membership of our society, and the often arbitrary distinction commonly drawn between what is thought to be right for them and what is claimed to be right for adults. In most discussions on how we should live, what people should be allowed to do, and which values should govern our dealings with each other, children are largely forgotten. I believe this enables us to cherish a false view of ourselves as a society of free independent individualists, owing little or nothing to anyone else, and we sustain this view partly because we do not think of children as being part of that society.

Of course we acknowledge that even self-sufficient individualists cannot have unlimited liberty, as one person's freedom limits that of another. Therefore, like every other society we have to decide under what circumstances it is justifiable to restrict freedom. I believe this problem is particularly pertinent to the question of how we should raise and educate our children because of the unequal relationship between adults and children, and the latter's relative powerlessness. However, once again, when discussions about the legitimate use of power or the right to liberty take place children are most frequently either not considered at all, or else dismissed in an aside. I am concerned to include children as members of our society and not to ignore them altogether or to assume, without examining the reasons for it, that they are quite different from adults.

In this book I shall consider briefly the question of what we mean by liberty, and then move on to questions of when restrictions of liberty are justified. My purpose throughout is to examine these problems generally and then to relate them specifically to children, considering the implications for their education, and for our education system. Thus, after asking whether we have a right to liberty, (Chapter 4) or examining whether paternalism is ever justified (Chapter 6), I go on to ask whether the same arguments apply to children. I then consider the implications of our beliefs about freedom on the upbringing and education of our children. Some people may wish to go straight to that part of the book, but I suggest you stay with me — at least until the end of the next section on what we mean by 'liberty'. Then go straight to Chapters 5 and 7–11 if you wish, and if you find yourself thinking 'What on earth makes her say that?' you will need to return to the earlier chapters where I hope you will find the answer.

What do we Mean by 'Liberty'?

Freedom as Absence of Constraint

The basic, minimal interpretation of 'freedom' as described by Thomas Hobbes is that freedom is the absence of impediment to motion[1], and this applies not only to people but also to stones freely rolling down hills. The traditional liberal view of liberty, however, is that liberty is to do with human beings, not physical laws or chance happenings, and that it is the absence of constraints deliberately imposed by human action. Isaiah Berlin, for example, says:

> Coercion implies the deliberate interference of other human beings . . . You lack political liberty or freedom only if you are prevented from attaining a goal by human beings,[2]

while Hayek calls freedom 'the state in which man is not subject to coercion by the arbitrary will of others'.[3] According to this view, if we are not subject to intentional coercion then we are free regardless of other impediments which may prevent us from doing what we wish, or what we might have wished had we known of the alternative possibilities.

Freedom as Action

A frequently expressed criticism of this account of civil liberty is that human freedom is too precious to be nothing more than a mere absence of restriction. It has been claimed in many different theories that freedom must be positive, active or, as Joyce Cary put it, 'Not an absence but a power'.[4] Although no two accounts of freedom appear to view its boundaries, its problems and dilemmas in the same way, many make a distinction between two types of freedom — a basic absence of constraint, and a more active use of freedom. Sometimes the distinction is said to be between 'freedom from' and 'freedom to', sometimes between 'lower' and 'higher' freedom; 'negative' and 'positive' freedom;[5] 'juristic' and 'moral' freedom[6] or between freedom as an 'opportunity concept' and freedom as an 'exercise concept'[7]. Although these various theories differ in significant ways they share the basic belief that, as Bernard Crick puts it, 'Freedom is doing something with it, not just sitting pretty on it.'[8]

Freedom as a 'Triadic Relation'

Faced with so many different interpretations of freedom, it is hard not to feel drawn to the simplicity of the claim made by Gerald MacCullum[9] that all freedom is (1) of some one, (2) from something and (3) to do or not to do something; and that what makes the difference is not that there are different types of freedom but simply that there are different 'somethings' that we may be free from and free to do. The questions which arise then are what are the important things we should be free from and free to do: what, in other words, are the significant actions that humans do value, should value, and should be allowed to do. Although, strictly, freedom is the absence of constraints to action, some freedoms matter more than others, and therefore some restrictions worry us more than others. Being forbidden to criticize the Government, for example, would worry me more than being forbidden to drive on when the traffic lights are red; and this is not because they are restrictions on different kinds of freedoms, but because of the value put on the forbidden actions. The freedom which concerns us most and which we strive to maximize is the absence of constraints to do the things that matter to us and achieve the purposes we consider important.

Freedom as Participation in Public Life

Another important traditional conception of freedom is that it is to be found in determining the conditions of the life of one's community by participating with others in public and political life. The free Athenian was not a man left alone to 'do his own thing' but one who was allowed (and was expected) to participate in civic life. This tradition, expressed more recently by Rousseau and Marx amongst others, is not much talked of today in our society which sees freedom as largely individualistic. Some of the dangers of overemphasizing this interpretation of freedom and neglecting the importance of the freedom to be left alone, were pointed out by Berlin.[10] He said it could lead to totalitarianism and an oppressive society in which individual liberty could be suppressed for the general good, and in which people could be forced to do what was said to be in their 'real' interests or accord with their 'true' natures, even though this might be at odds with what they say they want. However ideas do not have to be taken to extremes, and we can stop ourselves from sliding down slippery slopes if we are aware of the dangers. The freedom to control the circumstances of our lives should not be seen in purely individualistic terms. Joint decisions affect our lives as well as individual ones, and so participation in making those joint decisions should count as an exercise of freedom and restrictions to participation should be recognized as restrictions of freedom.

Freedom as Victory over Ourselves

It has also been argued that if external restrictions to human action count as limitations to liberty, so should 'internal' restrictions to self-fulfilment. Drug addicts and alcoholics, it is argued, are not free to do what, rationally, they would wish, and there are other disabilities and defects of character, which, it is argued, can prevent people from attaining their desires just as certainly as can external constraints. It is true that we sometimes use the language of freedom and coercion to describe people who are 'ruled by their hearts' or 'at the mercy of their tempers', but I would take the phrase 'passion's slave' metaphorically. The difficulty in extending 'freedom' to cover freedom from our personal inadequacies as well as external constraints is that it raises questions about what we mean by a self. If I am prevented from attaining a goal by a bully or a law then it is clear whose freedom is restricted. But if I cannot achieve my purposes because I am too easily distracted or too lazy, then it is not so easy to say whose freedom is restricted. It is the freedom of an idle person with poor concentration, or of someone whose real determination, perseverence and capacity for hard work have somehow been taken from them? Have we a 'self' which is quite different from the person our friends know, different from the person revealed in our speech and actions, or the person we know ourselves to be, yet is in some way more real and more truly ourselves? Would you or I be the same person (only freer) if we were, say, less shy or quick-tempered? I believe not. Our ordinary, normal defects, inadequacies and personal disabilities are part of ourselves. It does not seem to me to be right to equate our virtues with freedom and our vices with constraints. Of course I cannot stipulate against the broad use of 'freedom' for the absence of character defects or the pursuit of virtue. It is often used in this way — but not by me.

Freedom Is Not Just One Thing

One of my recurring themes in this book will be that we have many freedoms, some more valuable than others, and that there is not one thing, 'liberty', which is self-evidently valuable. We are so used to thinking of freedom as desirable and good that there is a tendency to skirt round the problem of undesirable or harmful freedoms and call them something else — 'licence' perhaps, or not 'true' freedom. However, freedom is also freedom to do harm, and that is sometimes harmful, undesirable and needs to be restricted. We are free when we are not restricted, and when we are restricted, then however necessary or desirable those restrictions may be, we are not free in respect of those restrictions.

Unintentional Restrictions of Freedom

In contrast to Hayek, who claims that freedom is restricted only by deliberate coercion,[11] I can find no good reason to deny that unintentional consequences of actions can restrict freedom also. If the caretaker locks the library not knowing I am still inside, then I am not free to leave, and though not blaming him, I am no less locked in than if he had done it on purpose. If I then shout out of the window to him, I would not think he would be justified in leaving me there all weekend on the grounds that my being locked in was the unintended consequence of a perfectly legal and morally unexceptionable act. I would feel that once the consequences had been pointed out to him he ought to come and let me out, and that if he did not, his act would not be the same morally blameless one it was originally. Similarly, once we know that certain social arrangements leave some individuals and groups unable to do what they and our society deem to be valuable, and what they are legally entitled to do, we are not in the same state of innocence that we once were. It is not satisfactory for us to say 'That is an unintended consequence of legal actions, and though it is a shame it cannot count as a restriction of freedom because we did not do it on purpose' and then carry on as before. We should either justify the restriction of their freedom or attempt to remove it.

There are not only two classes of actions; firstly the deliberately malicious ones, and secondly all the others which because they are not deliberately malicious must be morally unexceptionable whatever their consequences. What should not be forgotten is that the consequence of the 'same' act in different circumstances may be very different. An action cannot be considered good or bad, restrictive of freedom or not, solely with reference to the actors and their intentions and disregarding the consequences for other people. The question we need to ask is not 'Did someone fix things that way?' but 'Seeing that there are obstructions to free choice, could we arrange things differently and remove the obstructions?' If the answer to the second question is 'yes' and individuals or groups choose not to alter arrangements then freedom is being restricted just as surely as if that were the intention. If we see that social or economic circumstances, *that we could alter* prevent people from exercising important freedoms, then in altering them we will extend freedom.

Freedom and the Conditions of Freedom

As Berlin makes clear,[12] it is wrong to equate liberty with power, wealth or knowledge, and a mistake to confuse freedom with the conditions necessary for freedom. However, it does not follow from this that people are free regardless of how poor, ignorant or powerless they are, unless they are subject to intentional coercion. It may be true, as Hayek claims,[13] that a rich courtier living in luxury could be less free than a poor farmer. What this example shows, however, is not that there is no connection between wealth and freedom, or that a society which distributed wealth more equally would not find that freedom could be more equally distributed also, but only that wealth is not freedom, nor the only factor contributing to the enjoyment of freedom.

Freedom and Power

Freedom is not power, but nonetheless, the two notions are related. Not only is having the power to do something akin to being free to do it, but having power over others limits their own freedom to do what they choose. This is most clearly seen when physical force is used, but threats and 'undue influence' are also uses of power which restrict freedom. To offer people a restricted choice in place of an unrestricted (or less restricted) one is to diminish their freedom. There are also situations in which individuals or groups who have mutually incompatible objectives struggle to achieve their ends, and, if successful, may frustrate the intentions and restrict the freedom of the others. This may happen even if the loser does not have to do anything except put up with being the loser, and even if the achieving individual is unaware of the conflict of interests. For example, if a person or group has the power to close a railway line or bus route through a village then they restrict the freedom of the people who would have travelled that way had they been able to, whether or not the person or group are aware of their existence. The villagers may form an action group to fight the line closure and lose, or they may recognize that they have no hope and either move to the town or become more isolated in their village. It is not their choice of action that determines whether the Bus Company or its senior staff have power over their lives and are able to restrict their freedom. That power may exist even if there is no overt conflict or intention to restrict the freedom of others.

Freedom as Doing What We Want

Up to this point I have concentrated mainly on situations in which individuals or groups are prevented by human actions, intentional or otherwise, from doing what they want. However, freedom is not simply doing what we want. We are unfree not only if we are prevented from doing what we *want to* but also if other possible options are closed to us. It is possible, of course, that if we do not consider or attempt certain possible courses of action, we may be unaware that they are closed to us. Our freedom may have been restricted without our knowledge, and power exercised over us without any observable conflict of wants.

The extreme cases of determining another's wants — hypnotism and brainwashing — are widely accepted to be exercises of power which diminish freedom. More subtle forms of manipulation, I would argue, differ only in that they are harder to observe. As Lukes argues,[14] powerful people or groups may use their power to prevent certain issues coming to public notice and being discussed, and so avoid overt conflict. Secondly:

> A may exercise power over B by getting him to do what he does not want to do, but he also exercises power over him by influencing, shaping or determining his very wants. Indeed, is it not the supreme exercise of power to get another or others to have the desires you want them to have?[15]

Although it is possible to use power to create wants in less powerful individuals or groups, not all forms of persuasion and influence are exercises of power that restrict freedom. A clear and truthful account does not restrict freedom because it informs the listener of the way things are and of what must be considered when choosing what to do, but a misleading, distorted or partial account which persuades the listener that certain options are closed when they are not does restrict freedom. Clearly this does not apply only at the individual level. The use of the press, television and radio by governments (or others) for propaganda purposes is also an exercise of power which restricts freedom, because it prevents people from making decisions about their actions and opinions in the light of the fullest possible knowledge. If people do not know what is happening they are prevented from protesting about it or changing it as surely, and more effectively, than if protest demonstrations were banned. The lack of overt conflict between those in power and those kept in ignorance is a sign, not of agreement, but of restricted freedom.

There is a difference, sometimes a big one, between what we want and what is in our own interests. We know our wants, like our pains and fears, better than anyone else, and though they may be foolish wants, or have been created in us by someone else, and though we may be persuaded to change our minds, still, if we say truthfully that we want something there should be no disputing that we do want it, even though we might be wiser not to. Interests are different. It is possible for us to be mistaken about our interests, to want what is not good for us and conversely not to want what is. It is clearly possible also that an observer, perhaps better informed or more experienced, may be able to judge our interests better than we can ourselves. Because of this, those who value liberty and democracy face difficult decisions about restricting people's freedom to do what they want, and about requiring them to do what is in their interests. This is not simply a choice between liberty on the one hand and long-term benefit or safety on the other. If the expressed, but unwise, wants have been illegitimately created by others then their satisfaction is a dubious exercise of freedom. We have the problem that if our wants are created and our desires manipulated we are not free, and if they are disregarded in our own interest then again we are not free. The question of whether we are ever justified in making people do what is in their interests ('true' interests, 'long-term' interests) will be examined more fully in Chapters 6 and 7.

Conclusion

The traditional liberal interpretation of freedom is too narrow. It errs, not in saying that freedom is the absence of restriction, or that it can be restricted only by human beings and not by natural laws, but because its notion of human action is itself too narrow. Freedom may be restricted not only by deliberate coercion, but also by the unintentioned consequences of individual action and inaction, by the consequences of joint action and of social arrangements which are themselves not given, but the result of human choice and therefore capable of alteration. Our minds may be restricted as well as our bodies, and, as freedom involves the absence of restrictions on the satisfaction of potential as well as actual wants, it is possible for freedom to be restricted without our being aware of it and without obvious signs of conflict.

If freedom can be restricted by what we do and do not do, say and do not say and whether we mean to or not, then obviously restriction of freedom will be a more common occurrence than if it were brought about only by the deliberate action of a tyrant. It might seem as if our entire lives were spent oppressing our fellows. It should be remembered, however, that we do not have a moral obligation to remove every single removable obstruction to the fulfilment of everyone else's desires or possible desires. We are none of us entirely free, nor should we expect to be, and we do not have either 'freedom' or restriction but many different freedoms that we can enjoy to different extents. Some of these are much more valuable and important than others, and some are antisocial, undesirable, and ought to be restricted. I will be looking in later chapters at the questions of whether we have a right to freedom, and of what might justify restrictions of it. However, even though some restrictions are justified, and some freedoms undesirable, if our society valued freedom as much as it claims to, a wider interpretation of what counts as a restriction of freedom would not be resisted, and more vigorous efforts would be made to remove the restrictive circumstances of many people's lives.[16]

Notes and References

1. Thomas Hobbes, *Leviathan* p. 66 and p. 110
2. Isaiah Berlin, *Four Essays on Liberty.* p. 128
3. F. A. Hayek, *The Constitution of Liberty* p. 11
4. Joyce Cary, *Power in Men* p. 7
5. Berlin, op. cit.
6. T. H. Green, *Lectures on the Principles of Political Obligation* p. 14ff
7. Charles Taylor, What's Wrong with Negative Liberty? in Ryan *The Idea of Freedom* p. 173–93
8. Bernard Crick, *Freedom as Politics* p. 50
9. Gerald MacCullum, 'Negative and Positive Freedom', in Laslett, Runciman and Skinner (eds) *Philosophy, Politics and Society: 4th Series*
10. Berlin, op. cit.
11. Hayek, op. cit. p. 11
12. Berlin, op. cit.
13. Hayek, op. cit. p. 17
14. Steven Lukes, *Power: a Radical View*
15. Ibid. p. 23
16. As Marx said:

'The kingdom of freedom actually begins only where drudgery, enforced by hardship and by external purposes ends . . . The shortening of the labour day is a pre-requisite.'
Karl Marx, *Capital* 3/2 ch 48 section 3

It is not that a shorter working day guarantees freedom, nor that long hours were deliberately imposed to stop workers from choosing how to spend their time. The important points are firstly whether drudgery and hardship do have this effect, and secondly whether this condition can be altered.

Chapter 2

Consent and the Restriction of Freedom

In the previous chapter I claimed that even though we value freedom highly, not all freedoms are equally valuable and some are downright undesirable and ought to be restricted. I said nothing, however, about the vexed questions of who should decide which freedoms ought to be restricted and who should have the authority to restrict them. Ever since flaws were noticed in the idea that might is right, people have been trying to explain what justifies the restriction of liberty by those in positions of power, what makes their power legitimate, and what is the basis of the individual's obligation to obey a legitimate authority. One enduring explanation, known as contract theory, is that limitations of individual freedom are legitimate when people have agreed to accept them by forming a contract or covenant with their rulers or government. The theory is usually used to explain political obligation, but the principle can be applied to the relationship between anyone in a position of power and those who accept their power as legitimate. In the social contract people are deemed to have voluntarily given up some of their freedom in exchange for other benefits, especially the benefit of the security to be found in a law-governed society.

Contracting to Give up Freedom

The belief that the authority of the state is legitimated by a social contract has a long history, but until recently it had fallen into disuse. Rousseau expressed its fundamental premise when he said:

> since no man has any natural authority over his fellows and since force alone bestows no right, all legitimate authority among men must be based on covenants.[1]

However, contract theorists rarely if ever assert that people have *actually* contracted to give up freedom in exchange for other benefits. The social contract in which we give up our freedom and agree to obey others is said to be hypothetical rather than actual, and logical rather than chronological. There is no suggestion, however, that the criteria by which we judge actual and hypothetical contracts vary. A hypothetical contract to surrender freedom in exchange for security should be judged, then, like any real contract, on whether its terms were freely agreed and whether they were fair to both parties. Agreement alone is not sufficient to make a real contract fair to both parties, (even though it may make it legal) because it is possible that through ignorance or foolishness or for some other reason people might enter a contract freely though its terms were unfair to them or made demands on them to which they had no right to accede. Similarly a hypothetical contract to give up freedom will be considered fair only if it is thought that freedom is something that can properly be signed away, and that the benefits given in return are a fair exchange.

Is Freedom Something we can Contract Away?

The belief that there are limits to the amount of freedom that may be exchanged for other benefits is to be found in theories of social contract as different as those of Rousseau and Hobbes. Rousseau said that there can be no contracting away of freedom because it is essential to humanity.[2] (Actually Rousseau believed that freedom is essential only for *men*. However if 'to renounce freedom is to renounce one's humanity'[3] we must conclude that either it applies to women, or that women are not human. I favour the first conclusion!) Hobbes, on the other hand, thought that people would be prepared to give up a great deal of freedom for the peace and security that, he claimed, could only come from submission to an absolute ruler,[4] but even he said that not all freedom could be given up in a contract. He said people would be left with 'harmless liberties' — the freedom to do what was not forbidden, and 'true liberties' — a very strange list of things which no-one could, with justice, be obliged to do, (such as obey a command to kill themselves, starve themselves or confess to a crime, and allow themselves to be assaulted without resisting.)[5] So if, as Rousseau and Hobbes both believed, some submission cannot be justified even by a contract, and not everything that is agreed is thereby just, then more than agreement must be necessary to justify the exchange of freedom for other benefits. The obligation to obey a government cannot be justified solely by reference to agreement or contracts, even if that contract were real and not hypothetical. Underlying the contract there must be also, at the very least, the belief that political obligation and some individual freedom are things which may legitimately be agreed by contract. Contract theorists do not tell us the basis of this belief, and could not attempt to do so without admitting that the fact that a contract has been made cannot, by itself, be the conclusion of an argument justifying giving up freedom.

Contracts which Enlarge Freedom

Up to this point I have talked of the social contract as if it always involved people agreeing to exchange some of their individual liberty for other benefits. This is what is usually proposed, but the form of social contract conceived by Locke does not involve giving up freedom. It was based, Locke said,[6] on the laws of reason, and reason does not restrict us. Locke's difference on this point is due to the fact that he did not think that the contract preceeded social obligation, for he believed that people were already bound by the law of nature or reason on which the laws of the state were then based. He differentiated between society (which was natural) and the state (which was formed as the result of a contract) rather than between an aggregate of lawless individuals and a law-governed society. Locke's contract, then, is not taken to be the basis of an individual's obligations to his fellows: rather it is the means by which society is kept running smoothly and securely, disputes are settled and punishments meted out impartially. Locke also pointed out the role that laws can have in safeguarding and extending freedom as well as restricting it, calling law:

> not so much the limitation as the direction of a free and intelligent agent to his proper interest.[7]

It would seem that for Locke the notion of a social contract is unnecessary as an explanatory device. If people who already acknowledge obligations to each other and are aware that society would be safer, more just and more orderly if they cooperated with each other, gave up some of their freedom and submitted to the same laws, then a social contract cannot be the basis of their obligations. These will exist regardless of whether a promise is made or not.

The belief that a social contract involves exchanging liberty for other goods with which it conflicts is dismissed by John Rawls also, though for different reasons. In *A Theory of Justice*, he breathes new life into contract theory, and revives the debate. He puts forward the idea that people choosing the rules of justice for their society, but unaware of what their place in it would be, would give priority to liberty rather than to any other goods.[8] What Rawls means by giving liberty priority is that it may not be exchanged for any other social or economic goods, and that utilitarian ideas such as the public good or the happiness of the greatest number cannot be put on the scales and weighed against individual liberty.[9] The reason he gives for saying that people in what he calls the 'original position' would choose to give liberty this priority is that they recognize that we need freedom to carry out our life plans, whatever they are, and that it is therefore too valuable to risk losing it for ever or distributing it unequally.

Restricting Freedom to Improve Freedom

Rawls does not say that liberty should never be restricted: only that it should not be traded against other goods. He claims that liberty should be restricted only for the sake of liberty — that is restricting one liberty in order to enlarge or enhance another. This principle is meant to help resolve the conflicts that arise in real life, but it is when we try to give it practical application that we become aware of the difficulties involved. Firstly it rules out the possibility of restricting freedom on the grounds that it causes harm, suffering or injustice. Of course it is possible always to restate the ill-effects of these harmful freedoms in terms of liberty, so that a restriction on, say, theft or trespass can be justified because it increases the liberty of others to use their property as they wish; and a restriction on assault is justified, not because it prevents pain and fear, but only because it increases the freedom of the population to go freely about their business. However, my main objection to being punched on the nose is not that it would restrict my freedom, but that it would hurt. If we redefine all our values in terms of liberty then the principle that liberty can be restricted only for the sake of liberty becomes empty and useless. If every good is reduced to liberty and liberty becomes the only good, then the possibility of restricting it for other goods does not apply. What we need, when freedoms conflict, are principles which will guide us in our decisions of which freedoms should be restricted and which encouraged, and we do not choose between them as Rawls suggests we should, by seeing which freedom is the greater, but which is the more worthwhile.

As an example of liberty restricted for the sake of greater liberty, Rawls cites the rules of debate which give people greater freedom to put their points of view because they limit the freedom of others to interrupt.[10] However, as Hart says, it is

> misleading to describe even the resolution of the conflicting liberties in this very simple case as yielding a 'greater' or 'stronger' total system of liberty, for these values suggest that no values other than liberty and dimensions of it like extent, size or strength are involved. Plainly what such rules of debate help to secure is not a *greater* or more extensive liberty, but a liberty which is more valuable for any rational person than the activity forbidden by the rules.[11]

To decide which liberties should be permitted or why the liberty to punch or steal should be restricted we have to use some criterion other than the priority of liberty. We refer to other values: we look beyond liberty and its extent and consider the use to which it is put. To acknowledge that some freedoms are undesirable and others unimportant may seem to show a dangerously low valuation of freedom, reducing it to mere means to other satisfaction rather than an end in itself. However, the important freedoms that we value highly are more easily defended if they are distinguished from trivial freedoms, and are not encompassed in one indivisible whole called 'freedom', which is always more valuable than anything else.

Contract and Consent

If contract theorists wish only to set out the conditions under which they claim rule would be legitimate they do not need to show that there has ever been consent. However problems arise for those who wish to say both that consent is necessary for legitimate rule and that their present rulers are legitimate. They try to get round the difficulty by lookng for signs of consent other than the ones normally accepted for agreement to a real contract, and they claim to find them in tacit compliance, non-rebellion and acceptance of benefits from the state.

This presents a clear inconsistency in liberal social contract theory. It is claimed that agreement to the contract is like a promise, committing the individual because it has been undertaken freely. However, for a contract to be agreed freely there must be the possibility of not promising or contracting, and in the particular case of political obligation it would follow that those who withheld their consent to the contract could not be bound by it to obey the laws of the state. To overcome this problem the idea of consent is watered down, but in the process it loses its justificatory power. If everybody is assumed to have consented by not emigrating or by an act such as not rebelling or using the highway (even if they do not realize that these actions will be taken as showing consent) then giving consent ceases to be the rational act of free individuals who could withhold their consent if they wished. We may conclude either that obligation to obey the laws of the state exists only when undertaken freely (and therefore it has only rarely been justified) or that if we have obligations to the state these must be based on something other than free consent.

In most theories of social contract it is held that individuals' willingness to keep contracts which restrict their freedom is based on both moral and prudential grounds. If people are rational as well as self-interested, it is argued, they will accept limits on their freedom as long as everyone else does the same so that they can all enjoy the benefits of additional security. Once the contract has been agreed then, it is held, they are morally bound by their promises. However, one of the persisting criticisms of contract theory has been that promise-keeping is not something that a totally independent, self-interested, pre-social individual could either comprehend or engage in. In order to promise it is necessary to acknowledge moral obligations, and a person who was a stranger to the idea of being morally obliged to act in certain ways for the benefit of others would neither understand nor accept that inconvenient promises ought to be kept. If the obligation to keep promises is not accepted, then people would break them as soon as it suited them to do so, and, therefore, would give up no freedom.

The Isolated Liberal Individualist

The argument about promise-keeping is one aspect of a wider criticism of contract theory, which is that it is based on what Robert Wolff calls:

the classical liberal mistake of conceiving the relationship among men as purely instrumental or accidental rather than as intrinsic and essential.[12]

As Wolff says:

> Classical liberalism . . . portrays society as an aggregation of Robinson Crusoes who have left their islands of private value merely for the instrumental benefit of increasing their enjoyment through mutually beneficial exchange.[13]

The idea of free individuals making a contract to limit freedom presupposes this 'liberal' view of individuals and their relationship to society. The social contract is, as is always stressed, a logical construct and not an historic event, and contract theorists do not need to show that any such contract has ever been agreed before they can make use of the concept. Nevertheless, as it is a construct which is intended to help explain an aspect of the relationship between individuals and society (looking, as it does, for the basis of political obligation) it may still be criticized for its assumption that the free individual is logically prior to society. Contract theorists may not believe that there ever existed an individual, recognizably human but totally free and independent of society, but their way of talking as if this were so means we are led to look at the questions surrounding freedom and obligation from one perspective. Whether we consider Hobbes who preferred 'any subjection whatsoever' to what he saw as the only alternative, 'civil war and the right of the sword'[14] or Rawls who believes that liberty should have priority over all other social and economic goods, we start with individuals and their freedom and then move to the justification of their obligations. We are shown individuals who have freedom before they have obligations and who then choose to give up some of that freedom for something else they want more. Human beings are essentially social beings, however, and not just individuals who sometimes choose to leave their isolation, and so human freedom is neither logically nor temporally prior to social obligation, and our obligations are as natural as our freedom.

Non–Contractual Obligations

That there are non-contractual obligations becomes clear when we consider the different types of obligations that exist. My obligation to give a friend a lift to the station when I said I would is different from my obligation to look after my child, and both are different from my obligation to oppose an unjust government. The first is voluntarily agreed between individuals, the second is similarly the obligation of one individual to another, but not voluntarily agreed, while the third, also not voluntary, is an obligation towards all other members of the society, known or unknown. However, unless we accept the existence of the third type of obligation we could not have the first. For there to be voluntary, contractual obligations between individuals there must be at least one general non-voluntary obligation we owe to other people — that of honouring the obligations we have undertaken voluntarily. If our only obligations were the ones we have voluntarily chosen, then parents in past ages would have had no obligation to look after their unplanned children. Similarly, no one could be said to have an obligation to try to save a friend's life, or even treat their fellows with common honesty in their dealings, unless they had chosen to do so, and we could not be criticized for anything in our dealings with others except failing to carry out what we had agreed to do. The obligations of parents to their children, or, I would argue, of members of a society to their fellow-members, are not simply a matter of individual choice. Freely agreed obligations (like agreeing to obey the rules of a club when we join it) form a small section of a much larger range of obligations which exist whether we choose them or not. Society is not a club that we can choose not to join.

Political Obligation

To argue that obligations are inevitable and that the 'obligationless' individual does not exist still leaves us with the question 'Should I obey the government?' However now it will be asked by social beings who are aware of having obligations to the other members of their society and wonder whether obedience is part of them, and not by isolated individuals wondering whether it would suit them to give up their total freedom and commit themselves to some voluntary obligations. The obligation to obey authority, if and when it exists, is not based on a promise, explicit or tacit, to the rulers, but exists because co-operation in a just, law-governed society provides the way of carrying out our obligations to our fellow citizens, while engaging in a free-for-all does not. However, if our obligation to obey authority is based on our obligations to the fellow members of our society rather than to the rulers, it follows that our obedience is contingent upon those in authority pursuing the welfare of our society. Our awareness of our obligations to our fellows will not always make us compliant and may lead us to realize that sometimes we ought to oppose. We are not bound to unquestioning obedience to a government or other ruling authority simply because we recognize that we have obligations come what may, whether we choose them and whether we make a contract or not. If we accept this then we cannot abdicate our wider social responsibilities and leave everything to the government, but will accept the obligation to participate in the organization of a just society. We will reject completely Hobbes' idea that laws are 'the measure of good and evil actions'.[15]

Notes and References

1. J-J. Rousseau, *The Social Contract* p. 53
2. Ibid. p. 54ff
3. Ibid. p. 55
4. Thomas Hobbes, *Leviathan* p. 223ff and *Man and Citizen* p. 123ff
5. Hobbes, *Leviathan* p. 269
6. John Locke, *Two Treatises of Government*
7. Ibid. p. 347
8. John Rawls, *A Theory of Justice* p. 250, p. 302, p. 541–48
9. Ibid. 'The limitation of liberty is justified only when it is necessary for liberty itself, to prevent an invasion of freedom that would be still worse.' p. 215
10. Ibid. p. 203
11. H. L. A. Hart, 'Rawls on liberty and its priority'. in Daniels (ed.) *Reading Rawls* p. 239–40
12. Robert Paul Wolff, *The Poverty of Liberalism* p. 172
13. Ibid.
14. Hobbes, *Man and Citizen* p. 194
15. Ibid. p. 172

Chapter 3

Freedom and Democracy

In the last chapter I argued that people do not form social contracts with their rulers giving consent to the restriction of their freedom. It might seem, however, that although this is true of most political systems, a democratically elected government would be different. After all, the act of voting is a far more positive expression of consent than are tacit lack of protest, the use of common facilities or simply not emigrating. In a democracy, also, an alternative is available, and I claimed this was essential for genuine choice. However, even in a democracy people who do not vote are still held to be subject to the country's laws, and the alternative on offer is only an alternative within a prescribed framework. There is still no opportunity for people to give or refuse to give consent to the whole system, and so if we have an obligation to obey a democratically elected authority it is not because we have voluntarily agreed to do so. If this is the case, we may wonder what is the nature of the relationship that we feel exists between democracy and liberty? Other things being equal, are the citizens of a democracy more free than their counterparts in other political systems only because they have open to them the chance of choosing their leaders and replacing them when they become unpopular, or is there a more intimate relationship between democracy and freedom, perhaps based on the idea that in a democracy we are obeying the laws we have made for ourselves, and in so doing are still free?

The Freedom of Obeying our own Laws

Though we may as individuals sometimes choose to do something that restricts our future freedom, still, at the moment we make our choice I think it would be generally accepted that we are exercising freedom. We may choose to enter a strict monastic order, or enrol for an Open University course, and from then on our freedom will be less than it otherwise would have been. Yet if those future restrictions were known at the time we took our vows or filled in our application forms, and were accepted freely, then when we have to get up at the crack of dawn to pray or watch television we are obeying the law we made for ourselves and are, in that respect, free in a way we would not be if someone else had made us enter the monastery or the OU. However, although democracy is supposed to be 'of' and 'by' the people as well as 'for' them, there is a problem in transferring from the autonomous individual to the democratic society. We cannot say that when 'we' obey laws which 'we' have made, 'we' are still free, for the 'we' who do the obeying are a much larger group than the 'we' who make the laws. Thus the laws of a democracy or the rules of a democratic institution restrict the freedom of all those not involved in ruling or organizing in a way that our own self-made rules do not. Despite this, I believe there is a close interrelationship between democracy and freedom — though of a different kind than the rather simple one considered so far.

Participation and Democracy

I have argued that we are not individuals who can opt out of society if we choose, but that we are essentially social beings with certain non-contractual obligations to other members of our society, that are not simply the obligations of one individual to another. We have non-contractual obligations to society and to known and unknown individuals in that society, and I have argued that one of them is to cooperate in and contribute to the organization and running of a just society. Without suggesting that only people living in parliamentary democracies attempt to carry out this obligation, I do claim that it can be discharged most fully in a democratic society and that a truly just society would be democratic. The arguments about what would constitute a just society could take a whole book, so I shall simply assert that in a just society people would neither be in the power of others nor have power to use others, the welfare and interests of all would be of equal concern and basic human rights would be protected. To this end either the rulers would have to be saints or power would have to be distributed equally, so that people could have control of the decisions and circumstances of their own lives. In order to do this there would have to be the opportunity for people to represent their interests and put forward their views. The parallel with democracy is obvious, as is the extent to which present democracies fall short of the ideal. All human societies always will, of course for an ideal type is unachievable in reality. The fact that a society cannot be fully democratic or just, however, does not remove from us the obligation to make it more so.

Democratic Freedoms

If we are to discharge our obligation to participate and make our own contribution in the joint enterprise it will be necessary for us to be able to oppose what we believe to be wrong, dissent from some decisions and put forward individual and minority views. These freedoms are essential if we are to fulfil our obligations. In addition we must have knowledge. People cannot be involved in the making of decisions if they are uninformed, and so we must have accurate and relevant information on which to base our opinions and we will need to hear a variety of views, otherwise our contribution will be of less value. It is part of Mill's classic defence of free speech, of course, that people need to hear all sides of the question before they can make up their minds.[1] Sadly I am not as confident as Mill that truth will always triumph over falsehood and error, but clearly it cannot do so if it is unheard, and if information is suppressed or distorted people will not be able to come to a proper decision. Therefore a democracy will need a minimum of secrecy on the part of government, and a press that it is not simply free from government control, but is critical and not tied to a narrow viewpoint or sectional interest. There will have to be some restriction of individual freedom in a democratic society, as there always must be when people live together, because we cannot all be free to do just as we wish. However, if it is accepted that all have a contribution to make and an obligation to participate, then it will be necessary for many individual freedoms to be guaranteed also in order that we can carry out our obligation.

These freedoms are not just important freedoms that happen to appeal to democrats, then, or that can be demanded successfully by those who elect their leaders: they are essential for the existence of democracy, and essential for us to fulfil our obligation to our fellows to promote a just society. The relationship between democracy and freedom is not that democracy will give us or guarantee freedom, but that without certain personal liberties we cannot have democracy. Without education and information we could not take part in joint decisions, and without the right to criticize, dissent, protest, join with those who agree with us and seek to persuade those who do not we could not contribute our view of what our society should be like, or ensure that our interests would be considered. It will be apparent that in saying this I am using a wider interpretation of 'democracy' than is often used today and saying that democracy involves much more than voting for leaders who will do our thinking for us; more even than holding an occasional referendum on an important issue and then abiding by the majority decision. Democracy involves participation in the joint enterprise of promoting a just society, and a society that did not give serious consideration to the views of all its members would not be a just one.

Although lip-service is paid in western democracies to the value of democracy, there is no corresponding consensus of values and beliefs about the role of the individual in society and the relationship of the individual to the sources of power. The defining characteristic of democracy is generally taken to be that citizens are involved in political decision making, but some democratic theorists, such as Schumpeter[2] accept, or even recommend, that this involvement should be minimal and restricted to the choice of leaders. Schumpeter claims that the primary function of the citizens is to elect leaders who compete for power and then produce policies.

Democracy as the Choice of Leader

According to Schumpeter:

> the principle of democracy merely means .... that the reins of government should be handed to those who command more support than do any of the competing individuals or teams.[3]

If this is the case then, as I suggested earlier, the relationship between democracy and liberty would be simply that citizens of a democracy had a few more (or perhaps just a few different) choices that they could make. All citizens would be free in theory, and a few in practice, to stand in open competition for positions of power; all would have the chance to vote for an individual or team (though not necessarily one that represented their point of view) and all could try to vote out an unpopular government, but in between elections they would have very little to do but stand back and let the government get on with it. They would have neither an effective method of making their views known,

(Schumpeter is not enthusiastic about petitions and letters to rulers because these may distort their judgment) nor the necessary information available on which to make up their own minds about issues. They would be (or perhaps I should say 'we are') as Rousseau said, free once every four years.[4] Schumpeter would not view this as a disadvantage. For him, democracy is not basically about freedom to make the decisions that affect our lives, but about getting power and choosing who will be in power.

The Need for a Voice

The disadvantage for the ordinary citizen of a system in which their involvement is confined to the election of others (whether they are called leaders or representatives) or to voting in a referendum is described by Lucas. He says:

> A vote is a poor substitute for a voice . . . . It is not enough to be able occasionally to answer questions when we are asked them; we want sometimes to be able to pose questions, put forward proposals. What is important is not only the possession of the vote but the opportunity of taking the initiative.[5]

It is the desire for a voice that has always been the motive force behind demands for democracy. Though Schumpeter may use the word 'democracy' for the selection of leaders who will make decisions for us, choosing leaders is not self-determination, and it is the desire for this quite as much as the wish to choose leaders that prompts people to demand democracy. Early democrats believed that when decisions and rules were made that affected their lives, then justice required that they should have some say in their making. That has not changed. In any large group it will not be possible to satisfy all and make the rules and decisions exactly as any individual might wish, because there will be others who have different views and interests who will be affected too. However, when decisions which may affect us as individuals or members of the community are being made the democratic desire is to be able to influence them by contributing our experience and opinions.

To argue thus is to view democratic participation as a right, whereas I have spoken of it as an obligation. In fact it is both. We participate as individuals in order to protect our own interests, have charge of our own lives and concerns and avoid being in the power of others: but we are not simply individuals with individual interests and so we participate in joint decisions in order to make our contribution to the task of organizing a just society. Although democratic participation is an obligation, the first demands for it came from those who had suffered the injustice of coercion by a powerful government over which they had no control. They had been told their duty was not to participate but to obey and in such circumstances it is not surprising if democracy is demanded as a right rather than accepted as an obligation. Of course the decisions which affect and regulate our lives and may restrict our freedom and self-determination are made not only by central governments and so it is not only governments which need to be democratic. Rules impinge on people at many different levels and through different organizations, which may themselves be democratic, allowing their members to participate in the making of decisions that affect their lives and the formulation of the rules that govern their behaviour. A democratic society would not only have regular Parliamentary and local elections but arrangements so that people at work, the tennis club, tenants' association, trade union, school and home would be able to participate in making the decisions that affect their lives.

It might be questioned whether most people want to participate actively in the making of decisions, and suggested that those who do not are showing admirable common sense in not wishing to involve themselves in a life of endless debates and meetings. However, even if people are uninterested in national politics they are much less so about things that affect them more immediately, and the reaction to, say, the closure of a local school or post office is anything but apathetic. People are less likely to be apathetic if they have a realistic chance of influencing events, if the issue is important to them and if they have been socialized or educated to fulfil their obligation to contribute to the running of society. If it were generally recognized that we have an obligation to involve ourselves with matters of common concern, we would bring up our children to value participation, we would welcome any moves towards it, try in so many different ways to facilitate and encourage it, and, without spending all our lives moving from committee meeting to rally, the level of participation generally would be increased. It may be that those who take little interest in politics at present have realized that scant notice is taken of their views anyway and would have a different attitude if they thought their opinion would be given serious consideration. Perhaps they have perceived the current situation more accurately than those who attempt to influence governments, and their apathy is a rational reaction to the present distribution of power rather than an inevitable fact of life. It should not be assumed that mass apathy is inevitable.

Democracy and the Restriction of Freedom

When we have the opportunity to participate in the making of decisions that affect our lives we can express our opinions about what should be done, represent our interests and limit the power that others can exercise over us. However, there will still be occasions when we will not get our way and will have our freedom of choice and our freedom of action restricted. If, after all our participation and influence, we are still in the minority, and our opposition and dissent are unavailing, then we cannot be said to have made the laws that we are expected to obey. If we are not successful in getting our own way, despite having the opportunity to put our point of view, then our freedom will have been restricted and we will want to know if we have an obligation to obey a government which we did not choose and with which we disagree.

The object of democratic participation is not to enable individuals to get their own way, but to make joint decisions that reflect the common interest where it exists, and reconcile individual interests where possible. In any democratic group the contribution of all its members should be valued, and the final decisions will owe something to each contributor, even those whose views did not prevail and who disagree with the conclusions. Thus the disappointed democrats who participated in an open discussion will have contributed something to the final decision, even if the result was not quite as they would have liked. Unless the society is one in which certain individuals or groups constantly find themselves in a minority, the individual's freedom to influence joint decisions will be greater than in an undemocratic society, and even when the conclusion does not satisfy all, there should be greater understanding of why it was reached. However, after all that can be said about greater freedom to influence decisions, and greater understanding of disagreeable conclusions, the question still remains of whether we have an obligation to obey a democratic government when we disagree with it or believe it to be wrong, and the answer to this question, I claim, depends on what the government does.

The Obligation to Think for Oneself

It will be argued that if we reserve the right to decide when we should obey the government according to whether we approve of what it does, then we will have a chaotic society, or rather no society at all, but an aggregate of the isolated individualists of the liberal theory I have criticized. This is not the case, however, because there is an important difference between individualists choosing their obligations, and autonomous moral agents attempting to determine what their obligations to their fellows are and whether they can be fulfilled best by compliance with or opposition to government commands. Our obligations, like those of the government, are to the other people who make up our society. Sometimes, indeed often, we will carry out our obligations best by obeying the laws of the government of the day, but at other times we do it by opposing the government or even occasionally by disobeying its laws.

There is no reason to suppose that a society composed of autonomous moral agents would be chaotic, though admittedly it might not be as easy to rule as one made up of tractable, obedient citizens. Firstly, those who acknowledge the obligation to promote a just society will admit a *prima facie* obligation to obey the law, for without law the attempt to promote a just society would fail. Secondly, if the society is fully democratic there will be an additional imperative to respect the law, for the government will have facilitated discussion, listened to dissent and allowed protest, and so the final decision ought to represent the considered wishes of the majority. The majority is not always right, of course, and people are not always aware of what is in their best interests, but if one criterion of a just society is that it is organized for the benefit of all its members, then the fact that something is desired by the majority of them indicates it should be considered very seriously. Thirdly, it should be remembered that we reserve the right to disobey the law only when by obeying it we would fail to carry out our obligations to others. This is very different from saying we can do it when we feel like it, or find ourselves in a minority. Often we may be required to do something we would rather not do, and have not chosen or agreed to do, but unless our objections are that to obey the law would prevent us from fulfilling our responsibility to others, we should not break it.

As has been said, there is a *prima facie* obligation to obey the law, and so even when faced with what appears to be an unjust law, the person committed to promoting a just, democratic society would not consider the question of whether to break it in isolation, without regard to wider consequences, such as diminishing respect for the law in our society. For example, if we know that some of our taxes will be used to make nuclear arms and we believe that this is contrary to our obligations, we might decide that we ought to withhold some of our tax bill. However, there are more issues involved than simply the one of whether we should contribute to the building of nuclear weapons. The possibility of setting a precedent for others who did not want to contribute to the provision of schools or hospitals should be considered, as should the fact of whether or not a majority of fellow citizens wanted to build the weapons. Another consideration would be, of course, the consequences of breaking the law. Although we might hope, through our action, to draw attention to the fact that the particular law we had broken was unjust and should be changed, even a democratic government that was most sensitive to the wishes and needs of the people, would enforce the law as it stood, until the case for changing it had been accepted. Breaking the law is sometimes right, but, like other moral obligations, it cannot be done at no cost to ourselves.

The consideration of a wide range of factors rather than one simple question is part of what is involved in exercising moral autonomy, and we do not concede this right when we accord to a government a provisional right to make decisions on our behalf. We still have to decide whether our natural and non-contractual obligations to other members of our society are best served by obedience to the government of the day. We are not torn, as is sometimes suggested[6] between either obeying a government and thereby giving up moral autonomy, or remaining morally autonomous and therefore having to deny the right of any government, even a democratic one, to make commands. The mistaken premise on which this view rests is, I believe, that we have a government to do our moral thinking for us. This is not so. We have a government to help us organize a just society, and it should not be our ruler but our partner. Sometimes a democratic government will need to restrict our freedom for the benefit of others; (the question of whether it should ever restrict our freedom for our own benefit will be considered later) but it will also have to protect the important freedoms necessary for our participation in the organization of our society and the fulfilment of our obligations to its members. The restrictions of freedom imposed by a democratic government are not legitimate because we have contracted to accept them, or because they are expressions of our own wishes, but only if they are the necessary means of organizing society for the benefit of all its members. Even so, this may still sound like an acceptance of a dangerously high level of state interference in individual liberty. My claim, however, is not as careless of individual liberty as it might sound. It is a claim about the conditions under which restrictions of liberty *would* be justified if the government and the various agencies of the state were also striving to establish a just society. It does not justify every restriction of liberty which a government may claim is in the common interest. That governments may, and do, try to infringe individual liberty on the grounds that this is necessary for the organization of a just society when this is not the case is undeniable, but this demonstrates the fallibility or duplicity of those in government, and cannot be taken as a criticism of the principle. Nevertheless, it will be asked whether there are no limits to the restrictions the state may legitimately place on the individual in the name of the common good or in the interests of the other members of society? Have we no individual rights to liberty that the government cannot violate in the name of the greater good? Don't we have a right to liberty?

Notes and References

1. J. S. Mill, 'The peculiar evil of silencing the expression of an opinion is, that it is robbing the human race . . . . If the opinion is right they are deprived of the opportunity of exchanging error for truth: if wrong they lose . . . the clearer perception and livelier impression of truth.' *On Liberty*. p. 85.
2. Joseph Anthony Schumpeter, (ed) 'Two Concepts of Democracy', in Quinton, *Political Philosophy*
3. Schumpeter, ibid. p. 177
4. J-J. Rousseau, *The Social Contract* p. 141
5. J. R. Lucas, *Democracy and Participation* p. 46
6. Robert Paul Wolff, *In Defence of Anarchism*

Chapter 4

The Right to Liberty

In order to decide whether we have a natural right to liberty it is necessary to look first at what we mean by saying that we have a right to anything. There are many theories about the variously described natural rights, human rights and rights of man. The existence of natural rights has been confidently assumed[1] and equally confidently dismissed as nonsense,[2] from which diversity and disagreement we can learn little about rights except that if we do have them it is not in the obvious way we have arms and legs.

What is a Right?

The first, the least controversial and some would say the only meaning of 'rights' is to be found in a legal context. We have a legal right to have, do or not do what the law says we should be allowed to have, do or not do, and other people (either particular individuals or all others) have a corresponding obligation either to provide the object of our right or not to prevent us from attaining it. Often, however, the term 'right' is used outside the legal context, and refers to a moral right which may, in that society, have no chance of being upheld in court, and may be disputed by the majority. There is a limit, though, to the lengths to which the word 'right' can be extended, for even though rights may exist beyond the legal code, and beyond the moral understanding of all but a few enlightened people, they do not exist independently of human society. Even lone reformers claiming hitherto unacknowledged moral rights are appealing to a wider audience beyond their own country and generation rather than postulating the existence of metaphysical rights. Rights exist in, not beyond, a social context, and cannot be totally unacknowledged and unaccepted by anyone anywhere. Though this prompts the unanswerable questions of how many people must acknowledge a right for it to exist, or how long we should wait for it to be acknowledged, there is, in the notion of a right, some implication of others acknowledging the right and accepting the claim. Individuals claiming rights are not listing possessions, but contributing to a joint decision about how we should treat each other and making a statement about how we should behave towards each other.

Rights and Expectations

The idea that there must be a connection between having a right and having it acknowledged arises in realist theories which equate rights with expectations. These say that people have the right to have or do something if they have a reasonable expectation that they will be allowed to have or do it. Sadly, what we feel is morally due to us (our right) is often very different from what we may realistically expect, but there is a use of 'expectation' which refers to what ought to be, rather than what is. 'We expect children from *this* school to put their crisp packets in the litter bins', headteachers may announce at school assemblies, though experience will have taught them that realistically they must expect many packets to be dropped on the floor. They are using the word 'expect' for what ought to happen, and what could happen, though alas it might not. In this 'school assembly' sense of 'expect' human beings expect to be treated properly by their governments and not arrested arbitrarily and tortured — even though actual experience may have taught them otherwise — for they ought to be free from such evils and it is possible that they could be.

Rights and Moral Imperatives

If talk of 'expectations' and 'rights' is talk of what ought to be, the question arises as to what, if anything there is to the notion of rights beyond the idea of what ought to be. Is anything extra gained when we say 'I have a right to do this' or 'You have no right to do that' beyond what is expressed by 'You ought not to stop me doing this' and 'You ought not to do that'? Apart from in the strict legal sense of 'right' I believe that by talking of 'rights' we add nothing to the idea of moral imperatives. If we are imprisoned without trial and we claim the government has no right to imprison us and that we have the right to be set free, we are saying that the government ought not to lock us up without a trial and that it ought to let us go. If a torturer, having doubts about his job, asks why should he not torture, the answer 'Because people have the right not to be tortured' may sound like a reason, but it is really a restatement of the claim that he ought not to torture. I realise that to talk of rights in this way seems rather prosaic compared with the inspiring demands for human rights or the rights of man. However, I maintain that all such claims are basically statements about how people should be treated, and how others should treat them.

It might be asked why, if what I say is correct, we should talk about rights at all. We do so firstly because it is persuasive. When we claim a right it sounds as if we are giving a reason for being allowed to secure, or attempt to secure, the object of our right, rather than just asserting our claim. Secondly, the use of 'right' rather than the corresponding sentence using 'ought to' puts the emphasis on the person in the relationship who has the right rather than the one with the obligation. The sentence 'They have the right to a fair trial' focuses our attention more obviously on the individuals who might be denied a fair trial, in a way that 'Arbitrary arrest and detention without trial ought to be stopped' does not. Obviously what governments must not do to citizens, and what citizens must not have done to them by governments are the same, but focusing on the individuals with the right emphasizes their importance. It avoids the implication that those in power would shun the action for reasons of their own, such as that it would be demeaning for people in their position or would endanger their immortal souls. Thus when we say 'X has the right to Z' we are demonstrating that it is with X's welfare or justice to X that we are concerned, and not the moral health of others. We are not, however, providing a reason why X should be allowed to have or do Z.

Who has Rights?

Claims about rights are made for adults, sometimes for children, animals and foetuses and never for sticks and stones. There is much discussion about which classes of beings can have rights. Hart claims that there is a difference between having a right and benefiting from the performance of a duty[3], and that while babies and animals benefit from the fulfilment of our duty to treat them properly they do not have the right not to be ill-treated. According to Hart, if one person has a right and another the corresponding obligation, their relationship:

is not that of two persons bound by a chain, but of one person bound, the other end of the chain lying in the hands of another to use if he chooses.[4]

According to this idea people who have rights must be capable of choosing whether to exercise the right or not, and this rules out not only babies and animals, as it is intended to, but also the mentally handicapped, possibly the mentally ill, and those who are seriously ill or unconscious. To claim that my hamster has the right to proper treatment may seem to stretch the notion of rights rather far, but I find this less unacceptable than an interpretation which restricts rights to those who are healthy and bright enough to consider waiving them and releasing others from their obligations.

Hart's main point, however, is not about restricting right holding to the bright and healthy but to show that if there are any moral rights at all we have a natural right to freedom. The right is natural because if is not conferred or created by voluntary action. It belongs to all people just because they are people and not because they belong to a particular society or are in a special relationship. However, Hart does not take the view that because a right is natural it has a special status and is inalienable or imprescriptible. A natural right does not necessarily take precedence over other special rights. Indeed these special rights are a moral justification for overriding the natural right to freedom. For example, when one person uses his natural right to freedom to take something which belongs to someone else, the right to freedom is overridden by the owner's special right to keep what he owns. The owner's right is a moral justification for limiting the freedom of others to help themselves to his property. The special right justifies the restriction of another's freedom: a justification which would not be needed unless a natural right to freedom existed.

According to Hart:

> Any adult human being capable of choice (1) has the right to forbearance on the part of all others from the use of coercion or restraint and (2) is at liberty to do (i.e. is under no obligation to abstain from any action which is not one coercing or restraining or designed to injure others).[5]

Ronald Dworkin points out, however, that we cannot have a natural right to liberty, for liberty is a licence to do right or wrong, and we cannot have a right to do wrong.[6] Dworkin says that every law is an infringement of liberty, but we only protest that our right to liberty has been infringed in a limited range of cases. Many restrictions of trivial liberties are not considered important at all, which they should be if it is Liberty itself which is important. Dworkin gives the example of the creation of a one-way street and of restriction of free speech, both of which are restrictions of liberty but only one of which arouses complaints about the violation of individuals' rights. He puts forward the obvious suggestion that this is so because free speech is a basic liberty, but then says:

> However . . . if the distinction between basic liberties and other liberties is defended in this way, then the notion of a general right to liberty as such has been entirely abandoned.[7]

Clearly, if free speech is important and the freedom to drive up and down a one-way street is not, then it is not liberty in general which is valued and to which we claim to have a right, but certain particular liberties. As Dworkin argues, the idea of a general right to liberty creates a false sense of conflict between liberty and other values and provides too easy an answer to the question of why suppression of free speech is wrong. If we do not assume that we have a right to freedom as such then we have to probe more deeply to find out what we think is really important about free speech, and why it should be allowed.

Individual Rights and the Public Interest

As the restriction of some freedoms requires a much stronger justification than others, it cannot be freedom itself that is so valuable. The mere fact that a one-way street is in the public interest is reason enough to set one up and restrict individual freedom, Dworkin says, but to say that someone has the right to free speech is to say that he has the right even if it is not in the public interest. He calls individual rights 'political trumps held by individuals'[8] — a view similar to that of Margaret Macdonald who says that claims to natural rights tend to arise:

> when the plain citizen tries to make . . . articulate his obscure, but firmly held conviction that he is not a mere pawn in any political

game nor the property of any government or ruler, but the living and protesting individual for whose sake all political games are played and all governments instituted.[9]

I would agree with the point that individuals matter, must be considered, and do not belong to rulers or governments, but, as I have argued, they do belong to a society; though not in the sense of being society's possessions. I am unhappy with Dworkin's claim that individual rights exist even when they are not in the public interest, for our rights are what we should be allowed to do or have, and this cannot be decided without reference to some concept of public interest, or general good, and the rights of others. We cannot decide what individuals should be allowed, by the other members of their society, to do or have, without taking account of what the effect of exercising those individual rights would be on the rest of society, or on other individual members of it. However, this does not mean that all inconvenient individual actions can legitimately be banned because to do so would be in the public interest. Individual rights sometimes conflict with what it would suit the government, the state, or society in general to permit, but it does not follow that it would be in the public interest to override them. Rights are not individual possessions, but they are individual examples of what *everyone* should be allowed to do in similar circumstances, and so everyone has a selfish interest in preserving the rights of others.

For Dworkin's example of free speech, which he claims is a right even if it is not in the public interest, I believe it is necessary to have a conception of public interest that goes beyond the immediate issue. Even if what a person has to say may be judged to be not in the immediate public interest, suppressing it may be against that interest in the long-term. A precedent for silencing unpopular opinions, once set, could be used to silence opinions and facts that it would be in the public interest to hear. However, even an important freedom like the freedom of speech should not be seen as an inalienable right, for speech is action and actions have consequences to others. The wartime slogan 'Careless talk costs lives' had behind it the very reasonable assumption that when other people's lives are at stake we should not indulge in an excess of free speech. That and other freedoms which were generally thought of as rights in peacetime were viewed differently when circumstances changed so dramatically.

Inalienable Rights and the Minimal State

Rights and obligations which exist, not because they have been voluntarily agreed but because they belong to all human beings just because they are human beings, could be called 'natural rights'. However, to acknowledge that there are natural rights in this sense is not necessarily to accept that they are inalienable or imprescriptible and may never be overridden. This more extreme view is taken by Nozick who says:

> Individuals have rights and there are things no person or group may do to them (without violating their rights). So strong and far-reaching are those rights that they raise the question of what, if anything, the state and its officials may do.[10]

Nozick disagrees with Hart's claim that one of the special rights which overrides the natural right to liberty is the right of people conducting a joint enterprise according to rules to require submission on the part of others.[11] It is a right of this kind, Hart claims, which members of a society have over other members, but Nozick questions whether people who benefit from a social enterprise have the right to demand a contribution from others, even if they benefit as well. He asks why this should be, and what would be the case if the others do not benefit, of if they do benefit but would rather not, and he concludes:

> On the face of it enforcing the principle of fairness is objectionable. You may not decide to give me something, for example a book, and then grab money from me to pay for it . . . You have . . . even less reason to demand payment if your activity that gives me the book also benefits you.[12]

Nozick argues that there is very little the state may do without violating individual rights, and that, therefore, a minimal state limited to the narrow functions of protection is all that is justified. Although I disagree with his claims about the kind of state that is justified, his criticism of Hart's position requires further examination.

The Principle of Fairness

Hart says that apart from the natural right to liberty there are special rights and obligations which arise from voluntary actions, and that political obligation is based on one of these: the right of those who have submitted to restrictions while undertaking a joint enterprise to require a similar submission from others. Nozick argues that those who do not voluntarily take part in an enterprise are under no obligation to obey the rules. If, to use his example, a book is given to them, they have no obligation to pay for it and no-one has the right to take their money. Nozick's criticism of Hart appears reasonable because of Hart's insistence on the voluntary nature of obligations. If, however, as I have argued, obligations are not necessarily voluntary but are simply things that we ought to do, and if, as I claim also, one of our inescapable obligations is cooperation in the organization of a just society, then Nozick's criticism is not justified.

The Functions of the State

There is an irreconcilable conflict between my view and that of Nozick. It can be seen in the conflicting claims that the state may legitimately use its coercive apparatus only for protection against aggression, and the opposing view that one of the most important functions of the state is to promote the welfare of its members: it is apparent also in the claim that any form of redistribution (apart from reparation, which does not count as redistribution) is a violation of individual rights, and the opposing claim that a reasonably equal distribution of important goods is an essential part of a just society. The basis for these differences can be found in fundamentally different views of human beings, of society and of rights. On the one hand there are Nozick's individuals with rights of freedom, but no rights of recipience except those voluntarily agreed, who come together with others to serve their own purposes, and form a society which cannot justifiably require them to do any more than fulfil their contracts and respect the rights of freedom of others. Opposing that is the view of people as social beings, whose rights of recipience and rights of freedom arise, as do their obligations, within a social context. I can see no reason to start, as Nozick does, with individuals and one certain set of rights, and ignore the inescapable non-contractual obligations that arise from the mutual interdependence of human beings. It is not to undervalue individual rights to point out that historically they came a long way after the obligation to feed the baby!

What Happens when Rights Conflict?

Individual rights cannot be inalienable or imprescriptible not only because individual interests sometimes have to be subordinated, but also because on may occasions the *prima facie* rights of individuals conflict. Benn and Peters point out that, for example, in a famine one person's right to life might conflict with another's right to property. There are public discussions about the conflict between the right to strike and the right to work, the right to stage mass demonstrations and the right to walk peacefully to the shops or through the park. As Benn and Peters say:

> social regulation is a continuous process of adjustment between conflicting claims; the theory of absolute natural rights would seem to make the process impossible.[13]

For a case to be made for absolute rights it would be necessary to specify in advance all the exceptional circumstances in which the right would not apply. Thus we might say not that we have an absolute right to life or liberty but that we have the right except in *this* circumstance or when *that* happens, but we cannot know in advance what circumstances may arise. It might be claimed that we have the right to liberty, but when examined more closely the right turns out to be a right to liberty except when we break the law, or when our liberty clashes with that of others. We cannot specify in advance exactly what our rights are, because they are the things we should be allowed to do or have, and these vary according to changing circumstances.

Conclusion

If we take 'right' to mean the treatment that is due to people or what they ought to receive, and 'natural' to mean not specially created for any particular people but due to all human beings, then it could be said that we have natural rights, but not a right to liberty as such. We cannot have this right, because liberty is licence to do good or harm, and there can be no right to do harm. However there can be a presumption that people should be free to decide for themselves what they do in the absence of a good reason to restrict them. What will count as a good reason for restricting liberty will vary according to the liberty in question and the circumstances in which it is to be exercised. This is a subject on which there is much debate, and as individual members of society affected by the decisions, I would claim that we have the right to take part in this debate about what should and should not be allowed. Individuals do matter and should have their views and interests taken into account together with those of others when liberties and rights are discussed. However, it should be remembered that in saying that we have a right to contribute to the general discussion and have our views and interests considered I am not giving a reason why this should be allowed. To say that we should be allowed to contribute our views and have our interests considered and to say that this is our right are just two ways of saying the same thing.

Notes and References

1. For example, Spinoza, *A Treatise on Politics* p. 16
   'The natural right of all nature and consequently of every single individual extends just so far as his power extends; and therefore whatever any and every man does after the laws of his nature he does by the highest right of nature, and he has only so much right over nature as his power avails.' And Hobbes, *Man and Citizen* p. 115 'Neither by the word right is anything else signified than that liberty which every man hath to make use of his natural faculties according to right reason.'
2. For example, Jeremy Bentham, *Collected works* p. 501
   'Natural rights are simple nonsense; natural imprescriptible rights of man are rhetoric nonsense; nonsense upon stilts.'
3. H. L. A. Hart, 'Are There Any Natural Rights?' *Philosophical Review* 64, p. 180
4. Ibid. p. 181
5. Ibid. p. 175
6. Ronald Dworkin, *Taking Rights Seriously*
7. Ibid. p. 271
8. Ibid. Intro. p. xi
9. Margaret Macdonald, 'Natural Rights'. in *Proceedings of the Aristotelian Soc.*, XLVII, p. 225
10. Robert Nozick, *Anarchy, State and Utopia* Intro p. ix
11. Hart, op. cit. p. 185
12. Nozick, op. cit. p. 95
13. S. I. Benn and R. S. Peters, *Social Principles and the Democratic State* p. 96

Chapter 5

Children's Rights to Liberty

In the previous chapter I claimed that while we have no right to liberty as such, we have a right to — i.e. we should be allowed to — take part in the making of decisions that affect our lives and in the debate about how our society is run. I did not specify who 'we' are, and in this chapter will be considering whether children should be included amongst the right-holders, and if so, whether their rights differ significantly from those of adults. The subject of children's rights is one on which there has been much disagreement and confusion, some caused by different interpretations of what rights are and some by different views of how children should be treated. The problems fall into three broad areas: first there are the problems of rights in general, which were considered in the previous chapter; secondly, the question of whether children are the sort of beings who can have rights; and thirdly, if they are, there is the question of what rights they have.

Clearly the answer to the question of whether children have rights and if so what these are varies according to the interpretation of 'rights' that is being used. If the whole notion of rights is nonsense and they do not exist then children cannot have rights. If, as Hart says,[1] to have a right one must be able to choose to waive it, then young children and babies cannot have rights but older children would not be excluded. Disagreement about whether rights are legal requirements, moral imperatives or statements of idealistic aspirations will be carried over into the discussion about children's rights. Where children are concerned, the distinction between the right to *have* and the right to *do* (which Raphael calls rights of recipience and rights of action)[2] is particularly significant. People who are concerned with the former concentrate on the child's right to certain welfare benefits such as love, a home, toys, a free education, a nationality or whatever. The actual list varies but the emphasis is on what children should be provided with, whereas the alternative view is concerned with whether children should be free to vote, earn money, leave home or have sexual relationships. Again the list of activities varies but the emphasis is on what children should be free to do. The U.N. Charter of children's rights, for example, concentrates on their rights of recipience and says nothing about what they should be allowed to do.[3] The draft charter of children's rights published in *Where*[4] shares the U.N. declaration's non-legalistic concept of rights but is much more concerned with children's rights of action. Both these declarations would be criticized by those who hold that the identification of 'rights' with idealistic aspirations devalues the concept of a right. The argument is that rights are clear and definite and must be respected immediately and in all circumstances because of their overriding importance. They should not, it is said, be confused with something that is either impossible to arrange always and everywhere, or something desirable but non-essential which we might work towards at some non-specific time in the future.[5] *Where*'s draft charter makes it clear that it does not interpret 'rights' in the precise way, saying:

> a charter of rights is not a legal document. Nor is it a description of what can and will happen tomorrow. It is an ideal statement of how the world might be.

Clearly many of those discussing children's rights are not talking about the same things.

I have already argued in the previous chapter that to talk of people having rights is to make a statement about how they should be treated or allowed to behave. Furthermore it is to emphasize that the particular treatment is due because of a relevant feature of the person receiving the treatment and not because of the effect on someone else. Thus if we say A has the right not to be tortured we are saying not that they have a possession — a right — but that they ought not to be tortured, and also that B ought not to torture A because of some feature or features about A (perhaps human dignity and capacity for suffering) and not because torture is an unreliable method of extracting information, or that it will make B unattractively callous, or that the screams will upset C. When I talk of children's rights, then, I shall be talking of the way children should be treated or allowed to behave because of some significant feature or features they possess, and because of the effect such treatment has on them. Because this book is about liberty rather than rights, I shall concentrate on children's rights of action, their rights to liberty, rather than their rights of recipience but it is not possible to separate these completely. Sometimes rights of action are empty and useless if rights of recipience are not respected: sometimes there is conflict between them, as with the right to receive protection and the right to make one's own decisions. However, unless I state otherwise, when I refer to children's rights I shall be thinking of the things they should be allowed to do rather than what they should have.

Do Children have Rights?

The first question which must be asked about children's rights specifically, rather than rights in general, is whether children have rights. Since differences should be demonstrated rather than assumed the question is better tackled by asking why, if adults have rights, should children not have them, and, as I have already indicated, the answer to this question is strongly influenced by the interpretation of 'rights' that is being used. Using my interpretation it is clear that children do have rights because there are certain ways they should (and should not) be treated because of the effect this treatment has on them. If their rights are different from those of adults, and if their freedom is to be restricted in ways other than those which apply to the rest of us, then it must be because of some relevant difference in them, and not because it suits adults to treat them differently.

Rights and Obligations

As I have mentioned, Hart's interpretation rules out young children as potential rights holders. Another view which does this is the one which says that rights go hand in hand with responsibilities and obligations, and that as children do not shoulder responsibilities they cannot claim rights. However, although rights and obligations do go together, they do not do so in the sense that only those with obligations can have rights. The relationship is not that because we have obligations we are allowed to have rights, but that one person's rights correspond with another's obligations. Justice requires that those who want their own rights respected should carry out their obligations to others and respect their rights also, but we do not have rights as a reward for carrying out our obligations. There are, of course, special rights which may derive from the carrying out of special duties, such as the right to a week's pay for the person who has done a week's work; those who had not earned the special right would not have it. The claim that children do not have rights because they do not carry out obligations may be the lesser claim that they do not have certain special adult rights because they do not share the relevant adult responsibilities. For example, if children do not contribute to paying the mortgage, keeping the house in good repair, or enabling the bread-winner(s) to pursue a career, then it might be argued that they should not (as Harris suggests they should[7]) have a right to share in its legal ownership. However, even if this is so, all that is demonstrated is that the possession of certain special rights corresponds with fulfulling certain related responsibilities and it cannot be taken to show that children do not have rights at all. Even if it were true that children have no responsibilities and obligations this would not entail that they have no rights.

Children Sharing the Family's Rights

It is sometimes argued that children do not have rights as individuals, but only as part of a family, which, it is confidently assumed, is a whole with no conflicting interests within it. Acceptance of this view does not necessarily entail treating parents as the most important members of the family or giving them rights over their children. However, if it is argued that the welfare of the children is best promoted by allowing the parents maximum freedom from external interference in the upbringing of their children, then treating the family as a unit with no conflict of interest amongst its members will, in effect, give power to the parents. The view that the family is a unit whose interests are taken to be identical with those of the husband and father was once popular with those who argued against the emancipation of women. The protection of the more vulnerable members was said to be best served by denying them independence and by placing them wholly in the power of the most powerful member who had legal rights over them as well as economic and educational advantages. This argument is seldom heard nowadays with regard to women, as it is obvious that opportunities for independence give a better guarantee of proper and humane treatment than total dependence on the goodwill of another.

The argument is still used with regard to children, however, despite overwhelming evidence that some families do not serve the needs of the children in them, and that what many children need is protection from their parents or the chance to live away from them. For example, Robert Burt, taking the view that children do not need rights, says:

> children cannot be adequately or even sensibly protected by giving them the 'rights' that state officials will enforce against parents. Children can only be protected by giving them parents. The Children's Rights movement today is in danger of ignoring this simple homely truth and thus disserving the best interests of children.[8]

Burt argues that to speak of rights for children is to be legalistic, rigid and disinterested in situations such as the home and school where we should be flexible and passionately involved with individual children.

The Family and the State

Burt's reference to 'state officials' illustrates another dimension to the debate: the fact that it is not merely about the assignment of rights and obligations between two groups — children and adults. The adults are further divided into parents and the state, both of which may claim the right to act in the best interests of the child; the former claiming the right to raise children free from external intervention and the latter claiming the right to protect children from neglect or cruelty and to ensure that they are educated. Burt is aware that if children have legally enforceable rights these may have to be enforced by the state against the parents, and he fears that this will destroy what children need most — a close loving relationship with parents. In saying this Burt demonstrates the attitude to rights exemplified in the common phrases 'he's always standing on his rights' or 'she knows her rights' which suggest that to know or claim rights is to be somewhat aggressive and awkward. When we get to the point in a relationship when we start talking of our rights then, it is felt, it is clear that the relationship has broken down, for happy families and good friends do not resort to bills of rights.

There is a fear that acceptance of children's rights will result only in court cases and state intervention in family life, but though it is true that people sometimes have to make a stand and demand their rights, this is usually only a last resort. A general acceptance of children's rights would mean that compulsion and confrontation would be the exception, in the same way that a growing acceptance of women's rights means that women now go unremarked and unopposed into areas where once only those pioneers who 'knew their rights' would venture. It should be remembered that in an ideal world we would not need declarations of rights for adults either, not even laws against murder, so we should not exclude children alone from being rights holders on the grounds that claims for rights would be unnecessary in a good family relationship. Sadly not all families are happy, and although state intervention in a family dispute would not be the most desirable state of affairs, it is not demonstrably worse than the alternative of children being oppressed.

Apart from Burt's argument that children do not need rights, the other arguments against children being rights holders which I have considered have been dependent on a particular interpretation of what it means to have a right. Each argument could be rephrased more accurately in the form 'if having a right entails X then children do not have rights', and my criticism has been that having a right does not entail what has been suggested. My interpretation of 'rights' does entail that children have them, for clearly there are ways that children should and should not be treated for reasons related to the children and not to the effect on others. However, because of the wide variety of rights it is possible to have, to say that children are rights holders is to say almost nothing. The important question to answer is what children's rights are, and to do this it is necessary to consider first what rights adults have over them.

The question of whether adults have the right to make decisions for children and to restrict their freedom is made more complicated by the fact that the adults are divided into parents and others — usually the state or its various agents. Both, on occasions, claim the right to make decisions for children and to restrict their freedom to act as they might otherwise choose. Often there are disputes as to who has the right to do so, but the question I wish to consider first is whether parents have the right to make decisions for their children — not whether it is parents rather than the state who have that right, but whether parents have the right and their children have the corresponding obligation to obey. If parents do have this right, as opposed to sometimes being right to restrain their children for their own or other people's good, then actions which are otherwise morally neutral or even good would be judged wrong because forbidden by parents. The right to restrict children's freedom would apply not only to dangerous practices such as glue-sniffing or anti-social ones like playing the trumpet at dawn but harmless actions such as playing football in the park or joining the orchestra. Nor would it be necessary for parents to find reasons for their pronouncements: the mere fact that it was a parental requireme.1t would be sufficient to justify it. 'Because I say so' would be a good reason for anything.

The Moral Status of Children

According to Colin Wringe, the question of what is children's moral status, is fundamental to the problem of what rights adults have other them. He asks:

> whether children are separate and to some extent morally autonomous individuals who must remain temporarily in the care and control of others for purely practical reasons, or whether they are in some way inherently subject to an adult's authority.[9]

He concludes it must be the former, because the traditional arguments against children having the right or liberty to do what they choose (when it is not a wrong action in itself) are not convincing. The old answer to the question of why parents should have the right to expect obedience from their children was that they had given them life, and it was even argued that this gave parents the right to take their children's lives. Locke criticized this view on the grounds that the act of giving does not entail a right to take back again, and he pointed out that if giving life carried with it the right to receive obedience then this would last for as long as the parent lived, which would probably be past the time when the children had children of their own. Thus when children became parents they could not have absolute authority over their own children because they would still be in subjection to their parents.[10] Locke acknowledged the right of parents to 'honour' from their children but said this was not the same as a right to power.

> Honour thy Father and Mother cannot mean an absolute Subjugation to a Sovereign Power, but something else . . . What law of the Magistrate can give a Child liberty not to honour his father and mother? 'Tis an Eternal Law annex'd purely to the relation Parents and Children and so contains nothing of the Magistrate's power in it.[11]

Parents seldom claim the right to take their children's lives today, (though there are arguments about whether they have the right to deny them life-giving medical treatment). More often the question of parental rights over their children is about whether they should require obedience from their children, sometimes in such important areas as religion, education, employment and marriage, or sometimes in areas in which there is no question of the child's or anyone else's welfare being affected, but which are matters of parental preference. I would argue that there can be no right, as such, for parents to arrange their children's lives, restrict their freedom and expect their compliance, but sometimes parents will be right to make decisions for their children in the children's interest. To make out a case for parents having the right to the obedience of their children it would be necessary to show that children are incapable of making sensible decisions for themselves; that people incapable of making sensible decisions for themselves ought to have those decisions taken for them by others; and that the others who ought to take the decisions are the child's parents.

Setting aside the question of children's abilities as compared with those of adults until the following two chapters on paternalism, I will say only that acceptance of the above view would have consequences which would stretch far beyond the subject of parental rights and would entail the right of the knowledgeable to the obedience of the ignorant: unless, of course, it is thought that the parent's right to their children's obedience is justified not because of their irrationality or ignorance, but simply because they are children — a different class of beings from even the most foolish adult.

Are Children Persons or Property?

The idea that children are not persons in any meaningful sense often accompanies the belief that they are rather like parental property. This view can be seen in antipathetical attitudes to children's rights of action and to state intervention in family matters, and it is more often assumed than argued. If an argued rebuttal is needed, however, and the intuitive counter-assertion that people are never property is not sufficient, then Locke's criticism of the claim that parents have the right to rule their children is equally pertinent to the view of parents as owners. If procreation entailed ownership this would last until the death of the parent or until given up voluntarily. Therefore, if elderly parents do not own their middle-aged children, then nor do any parents own their young children. The proprietorial attitude towards children was also attacked by Mill who said:

> One would almost think that a man's children were supposed to be
> literally and not metaphorically a part of himself, so jealous is opinion
> of the smallest interference of law with his absolute and exclusive
> control of them.[12]

Mill was no champion of children's rights and he did not think they should
share adult liberties. However, he argued that the freedom for parents to
control the lives of their own children was not one of the important liberties
that should be guarded.

The belief that children should be treated as persons who should be
allowed to make decisions for themselves and not as the property of either
parents or state was one of the main tenets of the Children's Rights movement
which emerged in the '60s. The comparison of children with possessions has
been criticized as rhetoric by Wringe, who points out that though there are
laws restricting what we may do with our property these limitations are not
imposed in the interests of the property but in the interests of other people.[13]
Limitations on what we may do with our children, on the other hand, are
intended to be in the interests of the children, and so, Wringe concludes,
children are not treated as property. However, although it is true that children
are not regarded in exactly the same light as the television or even the poodle,
there are parallels.

Early legislation requiring parents to provide for their children was introduced not for the benefit of children but to prevent them becoming a burden to
the parish. Even if we now accept legislation protecting children against
cruelty and neglect or requiring them to be educated, these laws were all criticized when they were first introduced as an intrusion into family life and as
destructive of parental control. It appears to be generally accepted also that
parents may restrict their children's freedom in ways that no adult would
accept and not only in circumstances in which it is in the children's own
interest or to prevent harm to others. (One would need an unusually broad
interpretation of 'children's interests' and 'harm to others' to include all
arbitrary parental prohibitions and requirements.) Thus while it would be an
exaggeration to say that children are treated as if they were parental property
and nothing else, it is true that they are often treated more like possessions
(even if cherished and pampered ones) than individuals with their own lives to
lead and their own ideas on how they wish to lead them.

Parents' Rights

Despite the fact that Mill, convinced libertarian that he was, argued that parents should have less liberty and not more with regard to the upbringing and education of their children, and that emphasis should be placed on parents' responsibilities towards their children rather than on their rights over them, the claim that the state should not intervene in family life was argued then and is still argued today on libertarian grounds. Libertarians are in somewhat of a dilemma (though they do not always seem to realize this) because on the one hand they are in favour of people having control of their own lives and not being coerced by others, but on the other hand one of the freedoms they value most highly is for adults to bring up their children as they wish without the intrusions of the state. They do not acknowledge the fact that state 'intrusion' may safeguard children's freedom, while freedom for parents may restrict the freedom of children to the point of oppression. In the argument between parents and state over who has the right to decide what is in the best interests of the child, the children's own opinions are usually overlooked.

It is sometimes argued[14] that as the right to bear and raise children is such a fundamental liberty it cannot be overridden in the best interests of the child. I believe, however, that there is some confusion between two ways in which we might have the right to bear and raise children. We have that right, but we have it in the same way we have the right to marry — the state should not stop us if we are able to do it: but having children, like marrying, involves others who also have rights. No-one would suggest that we have the right to marry anyone we want to regardless of the opinion of the person we have chosen, yet it is claimed that not only should parents be able to raise children as they wish, free from the interference of the state, but that the other partner in the re-lationship — the child — should have no say in the matter either. As increased divorce and questions of custody have forced us to realize, when the decision is as important as where and with whom the child should live the question should not be 'Who has the right to the child?' but 'What does the child want?' or 'What is in the child's best interest?' If the child is old enough to understand the issue and have a valid opinion on it then that opionion should not be over-ruled on the grounds that someone else has rights over the child. The welfare of children is not the only concern of society or individuals within that society, but it has an extremely high priority. When, in sad cases, a choice has to be made between unhappy children and unhappy parents the decision should not be made in favour of the adults on the grounds of their parental rights.

Protection, Guidance and the Child's Interest

If the justification for adults ever having the right to override children's wishes and make decisions for them is that this is in children's interests because they need protection and guidance, then adults' rights to make decisions for children should be limited to making decisions in children's interests and to the provision of the necessary protection and guidance. Their rights will not extend to rights over children, regardless of what is in children's interests. In saying this I am not assuming that questions of what is in children's best interests and whether they are capable of understanding fully the issues involved in making a decision are unproblematic. They are far from that, but however difficult the application may be in certain cases the principle is simple. If adults have the right to make decisions for children on the grounds that children do not understand what is at stake and do not appreciate, as adults do, what is in their best interests, then, firstly, if children do understand the issues and can perceive their interests correctly, adults' rights to make decisions for them must cease, and secondly, the decisions which adults make for the children must be in the children's interests, and not for the adults' convenience.

Should Children have the same Rights and Liberties as Adults

If children are not possessions but persons with plans and purposes of their own, it must be asked whether there is any reason why they should not be as free to carry out those plans as adults are. As was stated earlier, if children's rights are different from those of adults this must be because of some relevant difference between children and adults, and the question is whether age constitutes such a relevant difference. At first glance age alone does not appear to be the sort of difference that justifies differential treatment. Like sex or race it is beyond the control of the individual and it is but one characteristic shared by people who are in other respects very different from each other.

Most frequently it is argued that it is not children's age alone that makes it right for adults to restrict the liberty of children and for children's rights to be defined differently from those of adults, but the accompanying charac-teristics of dependency, irresponsibility and irrationality. However, we are all dependent to some extent on others, and elderly and handicapped people are particularly so, but it is not suggested that their rights to liberty should be different from those of other adults, except in extreme cases. Irresponsibility and irrationality are often found in adults, so if it is possession of those characteristics which makes restrictions of liberty legitimate then there are many adults who should be restricted. As Harris says:

> If freedom from control and full political status are things we qualify for by acquisition of a range of capacities then as soon as anyone possesses those capacities they qualify and if they never acquire them they never qualify.[15]

He concludes that we do not qualify for political or other personal liberties on account of our capacities and so we have no right to deny freedom from control or the right to vote to children on the grounds that they lack them. If we do not wish to be stricter with adults, it should be considered whether we should lower the voting age or abolish it altogether.

It has been suggested that children should be allowed to vote or partake in other adult activities as soon as they are ready,[16] which, in the absence of qualifying examinations, would be as soon as they feel themselves to be ready. There is no one conclusive argument against this point of view, but there are several contributary reasons why I think it would not be right to free children entirely from all the restrictions which do not apply to adults. If children are to be allowed to vote, be sexually active, work for money, and choose whether to attend school we must acknowledge and deal with the problem that they may be manipulated or pressurized by adults. Children, at least while they are smaller and less articulate than adults are vulnerable to adult attempts to coerce and manipulate them. Holt, who argues for children to be allowed to share adult rights, claims that a society which agreed to give children the vote and other adult freedoms would not be the sort of society in which adults would manipulate, coerce or pressurize children,[17] but I find this argument unsatisfactory.

It seems foolish to argue for specific changes in the way our society is organized, on the grounds that we are extremely unjust to children, and then trust that there will be a corresponding change of spirit in every adult in that society. It is wiser, surely, to follow Rousseau's advice and take men as they are and laws as they might be. Sadly some men and women, as they are, are likely to use children in ways that are not in the children's interests, and this will not change simply because the law does. We have abolished the death penalty but people still gather at the scene of a murder trial to shout abuse at the defendant, showing that a change in the law does not necessarily bring about a different attitude. Similarly we might extend suffrage and other adult rights to children, but this would not necessarily bring all adults to see that children should be treated as individuals with equal rights of choice. Holt tells us of the cruelty of parents to their children and of the number who maltreat, murder and neglect them; yet his response to the fears that some parents may coerce their children to vote a particular way or exploit their labour if they were allowed to work is that such sentiments are 'snobbish and hypocritical.'[18] This position is inconsistent. Those who are concerned enough about children to want to extend their rights and freedom should ensure that they do not leave children with less effective freedom, and adults with more opportunities to use their power over children unofficially. A wholesale extension of adult rights to children would give children some freedoms they may not understand, and could place them even more securely in the power of individual adults who wish to exploit them.

Understanding and Rights of Action

The notion of understanding is relevant to the question of children's rights because to say we have a right to do X is to say we should be allowed to do X if we choose, and we cannot be said to have chosen to act in a particular way if we do not understand something of the meaning of the action and what the choice entails. If children are to be free to choose to take on adult rights and take part in the debate about how our society should be run, then they must have some understanding of these rights and the issues being debated, or what they do when they opt to vote or leave home, or have a sexual relationship with an adult will not be a free act. If we consider, for example, the act of voting, it will be acknowledged that voting is not simply putting a cross by a name. It is an action with a meaning. While it is not necessary to know all the political implications of a particular vote, unless a person understands the meaning of putting a cross by a name they are not voting. So we might give children the right to enter a polling booth and place a cross by a name from the first moment they could hold a pencil, but until they understand what they are doing they will not be voting. I have often carried out votes in infant classes to decide such issues as which songs to include in the end of term concert and the elections can be chaotic. Many children do not understand that they are being asked to choose *between* alternatives so their hands shoot up for every song they like, and if I manage to clamp down on that electoral malpractice the first song on the list always wins. The minority who do not like the final choice are uncomprehendingly aggrieved because they thought we were choosing their favourite song and they cannot understand how something they do not like can be their favourite song! For all its apparent simplicity voting does not come easily to the under sevens, and to extend the right to vote to this age group would do nothing more than give an extra vote to the parents who could coach their children on where to place their cross.

I have spoken, however, of young children, and of a wholesale extension of adult rights to them. The argument does not extend to older children who understand what they are doing and are less likely to be coerced by their parents or other adults. The problem still arises, of course, of how to decide when people should assume adult rights. What must decided is whether there is greater injustice in denying adult rights to all children below a certain age, allowing them to those who pass a qualification test, or allowing them to all, including those unable to understand or exercise them. If age is the criterion that is chosen then any age that is fixed upon will discriminate unfairly against those below the age who would be capable of exercising their rights wisely. Harris says that:

> We must remember that to deny someone control of their own lives is to offer them a most profound insult, not to mention the injury which the frustration of their wishes and the setting at naught of their own plans for themselves will add. Perhaps we should conduct annual examinations from an early age to be sure that we do as little of this sort of damage as possible?[19]

However, I would suggest that the insult and injury would be greater from being examined and judged inadequate than from being judged too young.

Qualifying for Adult Rights

If tests in political knowledge were introduced there would be the danger that any test to find out who was sufficiently well-informed about political issues to be trusted with a vote might discriminate against a section of the community — most probably the poor and ill-educated. This would substitute one injustice for another. If people had to qualify for adult rights, then unless a test could be devised that was more accurate and free from human error and bias than any test has ever been, there would be instances of injustice through misapplication of the test. Even if testing techniques were vastly improved and the possibility of corruption could be eliminated, individuals and groups would still be treated unjustly under such a system because they would be denied rights and excluded from playing their part in their society by other members of that society imposing their own standards and values. There is a manifest injustice in excluding people from so many important areas of private and public life on grounds which others have selected and which the rejects have no chance to change. If all members of a society should have the same basic rights to make decisions regarding their private lives and participate in public life, then children too must be allowed these same rights. But this entails giving rights to some children who will not understand what is involved and it carries the risk that relaxing the laws about what children are allowed to do may place them more securely in the power of individual adults who are in a position to control them.

Is a Shared Injustice Less Unjust?

The argument that restricting children more than adults is not unjust because children will be granted adult rights eventually has been much criticized.[20] It is rightly pointed out that imprisoning everyone for several years could not be justified on the grounds that it is *everyone* who is imprisoned and that eventually they will all be released, and that individual instances of injustice do not cease to be injustices when they are multiplied. However, there is a sense in which a deprivation equally shared is considered to be less unfair than one meted out to a few individuals or groups, particularly if it is felt to be necessary. National Service, however much it was disliked by those who had to do it, was considered less unfair than the American draft for the Vietnam war which drew most heavily on the unemployed and those without college education. Similarly I would argue that restrictions on children's freedom which are necessary to protect those who need it are less unfair when they are shared by all than they would be if attempts were to be made to sort out the competent from the incompetent.

Discrimination on the grounds of age is rough and ready: it does not distinguish between those who are rational and mature in outlook, who drink moderately, have responsible sexual relationships and who are fortunate in having parents who would not exploit them, and those others who need protection from adults and from their own inexperience. In this it is less than just to some individuals. The inflexibility of law, however, is not confined to the question of children's rights. Laws are general and therefore cannot make fine discriminations and though this is sometimes cause for concern when we feel that particular extenuating circumstances should be taken into account, it is also one of the strengths of laws. Their generality rules out partiality and arbitrary judgments. They have, at least, the virtue of letting us know where we stand, and although laws relating to the age at which we are allowed to do certain things restrict our freedom, they also make it clear that after the stated age we are free to do those things. We do not usually have to prove we are capable or make out a special case and hope for a favourable judgment: we have our adult rights simply because we have lived a certain number of years. Discrimination on the grounds of age, unlike discrimination on the grounds of sex or race is not imposed by one group on another cohesive group. In consists of restrictions to which we are all subject at one stage of our lives and from which almost all of us escape. If these restrictions are necessary to protect children from worse injustice then I believe they are justified. The crucial question, then, is whether some restrictions are necessary for children in addition to those imposed on adults.

Children's Rights to Protection

Despite remarkable stories of children surviving without adult help it is still the case that because of their size, inexperience and less-developed rationality they are more vulnerable than most adults and need protection and guidance. No-one would deny that this is true of babies, but one of the many problems to do with children is that they grow in the experience and understanding necessary to exercise adult rights and withstand adult manipulation only gradually. Holt argues that what children need are not special rights and protection but the same rights and protection as the rest of us:[21] the protection of the law and the right to sue those who damage our interests. However, though I would agree that this would sometimes help to protect children, I believe they need additional protection, because the inexperience which might make them vulnerable to those who wish to exploit them would also be a disadvantage when they tried to claim their rights. The probability is that they would not be able to assert their ordinary rights as citizens even as effectively as adults can. If children have special needs and disabilities related to their age, then it is no more unjust to ensure that these needs are met than it is to discriminate in favour of other people who are handicapped in some ways and ensure that their particular needs are met. Lack of the capacity for rational choice is a handicap which prevents people from having an equal chance of pursuing their goals, and so it has been argued that restricting the liberty of those who are handicapped in this way is not to impose a burden on them, but to provide them with a benefit of protection and guidance.[22]

Restricting children's freedom, then, in ways different from those in which adults' freedom is restricted must be in response to the child's need. Of course, the concept of need is itself problematic, and most adults who restrict children's freedom say (and sometimes really believe) that they are doing it for the child's own good. If individual circumstances are to be taken into account then important decisions in children's lives will be left to individual adults, because general rules cannot be found that will apply to all children. This obviously leaves the grounds for decisions on restricting children's freedom rather vague, and there will be much scope for individual value judgments. However, laws stipulating that all children should or should not be allowed to do X could not take into account the maturity and capabilities of individual children. Inevitably, if we accept that children's freedom should ever be restricted there will be disagreement about when that restriction is justified, because decisions on the important factors — the children's needs, interests and ability to choose rationally for themselves — are subjective.

Children do not become rational individuals with plans and purposes of their own at one obvious point in their lives: they do so gradually, and are able to make sensible choices in some areas before they can do so in others. We know that making mistakes has educational value, and so children should sometimes be given the opportunity to learn from their own mistakes, but sometimes the dangers of allowing children to make their own decisions and mistakes will be judged to be too great. Therefore many of the arguments about children's rights are not about whether children are inherently subject to adults and whether as a group they should have any rights of action, but about the age at which they should be free to make certain decisions. Should twelve year-olds be allowed to choose to have their ears pierced, be tattoed or buy cigarettes? Should people of fourteen choose the subjects they study at school, or even whether they have to go to school at all? These are examples of the many questions asked about children's rights, and the children's rights campaigners correctly stressed that 'childhood' today is now prolonged far beyond what was normal only one or two centuries ago. Without wishing to suggest that previous generations were right to fix the age at which people could start work at twelve, seven or even three, the existence of different standards should at least make us question our own and consider whether children ought to be allowed greater liberty to make their own decisions.

Conclusion

If restriction of children's freedom were based solely on genuine need and the promotion of children's interests, I believe it would be less extensive than is common today. There would be certain areas of choice (personal appearance for example) where there was no question of harm to the child, which could be extended even to the youngest children capable to expressing a preference, and others where the recognition that people between the ages of, say, twelve and eighteen have more in common with adults than younger children would lead to an extension of their rights of action. However, sometimes children will need to be protected from themselves and the consequences of their own actions, and then adults will be obliged to restrict children's freedom. Knowing that there is no perfect solution, concerned adult members of a society will be aware that new laws may be necessary to protect children, or that old ones no longer serve their original purpose and should be changed. If children need protection and guidance beyond that needed by most adults, and if adults have an obligation to provide this, then we can say that children have a right to this protection, and a right to have their liberty restricted.

Notes and References

1. H. L. A. Hart, 'Are There any Natural Rights?' *Philosophical Review* 64, 1955
2. D. D. Raphael, *Problems of Political Philosophy* p. 68
3. U.N., U.N. Declaration of the Rights of the Child. in Onora O'Neill, *Having Children* p. 112
4. A.C.E., *Where* No. 56 p. 105
5. See Maurice Cranston, 'Human Rights real and supposed'. in Raphael, *Political Theory and the Rights of Man* p. 43–53
6. A.C.E., op. cit.

7. John Harris, 'The Political Status of Children'. in Graham, *Contemporary Political Philosophy* p. 53

8. Robert A. Burt, 'Children as Victims'. in Vardin and Brody, *Children's Rights: Contemporary Perspectives* p. 51

9. C. A. Wringe, *Children's Rights* p. 98

10. John Locke, *1st Treatise of Government* Para 64 p. 224

11. Ibid.

12. J.S. Mill, *On Liberty* p. 174

13. Wringe, op. cit. p. 94

14. See, for example Rene K. Ulliver, 'Children Versus Parents: Perplexing Policy Questions for the ACLU' in O'Neill op. cit. p. 128

15. Harris, op. cit. p. 37

16. See, for example, Harris, op. cit. and John Holt, *Escape from Childhood* p. 15

17. Ibid, p. 144

18. Ibid, p. 185

19. Harris, op. cit. p. 49

20. See for example Julia Rosenak, 'Should Children Be Subject to Paternalistic Restrictions on Their Liberties?' *Journal of the Philosophy of Education Society* vol 16 p. 89–97

21. Holt, op. cit. p. 178ff

22. Laurence D. Houlgate, 'Children, Paternalism and Rights to Liberty.' in O'Neill op. cit. p. 273

Chapter 6

Paternalism

According to J. S. Mill:

> the only purpose for which power can rightfully be exercised over any member of a civilized community against his will is to prevent harm to others. His own good, either physical or moral is not a sufficient reason. He cannot rightfully be compelled to do or forbear because it will be better for him to do so, because it will make him happier, because in the opinion of others it would be wise or even right.[1]

In this chapter I want to consider this claim. I shall suggest that we are sometimes justified in compelling or restraining others in their own interest and that we have responsibilities to them beyond those of trying to persuade them or leaving them alone. Like all moral judgments this cannot be proved, but if we were to say that paternalism is always wrong, the consequences would be far-reaching. Imagine a society in which it was considered unjustified to do any of the following: stop a three year-old child from drinking bleach, a twelve year-old from going on a glue-sniffing binge, an intoxicated or furious friend from writing a letter of resignation, or a mentally retarded person from signing a damaging contract.

In fact, although Mill claims that his one simple principle is that prevention of harm to others is the only purpose for which power can rightfully be exercised, he too admitted some exceptions (children and people from 'backward countries') and, once exceptions to the general rule have been made, it is necessary to say in what relevant way these are different, and then to accept that whenever and wherever similar relevant differences exist they will also be exceptions to the rule. Mill does not go into these details (and nor shall I until the next chapter) but simply asserts that paternalism for minors and backward peoples is justified because 'Those who are still in a state to require being taken care of by others must be protected against their own actions as well as against external injury.'[2] We do not have to suppose that Mill thought anyone under twenty-one or from a 'backward nation' was incapable of choosing their life plans rationally while everyone over twenty-one from a 'civilized' nation did nothing else. His purpose in writing *On Liberty* was not to discuss the problem of just when people become rational, or even what to do with the minority who never do, but to make a plea for freedom from interference for adults, most of whom are fairly rational most of the time.

Mill's modified claim, then, is that paternalism is never justified for civilized adults, but even this is unusually strong and definite for Mill whose pronouncements are usually hedged round with qualifications. I believe it is too strong, being based on an overconfident assumption that as individuals we know, when we make choices, what the consequences of our choosing might be. As was argued in Chapter 1, what looks like a free choice may be the result of subtle manipulation or undue influence as well as plain ignorance. Hart points out, rightly, that since Mill's time there has been:

> a general decline in the belief that individuals know their own interests best, and . . . an increased awareness of factors which diminish the significance to be attached to an apparently free choice.[3]

He accuses Mill of mistakenly endowing people with:

> too much of the psychology of a middle-aged man whose desires are relatively fixed, not liable to be artificially stimulated by external influences; who knows what he wants and what gives him satisfaction or happiness; and who pursues these things when he can.[4]

In fact we do not have to look far to find people doing things which will make them unhappy, and if this is the case then a utilitarian such as Mill should be in favour of some intervention which will prevent unhappiness. However, Mill was not a consistent utilitarian on this point, his concern for liberty being so great that he felt coercion was not justified even if it did make people happier. To be consistent a utilitarian who disapproved of paternalism would have to argue that, *a priori*, the happiness of being allowed to go to the devil in one's own way is always greater than any happiness that might follow from paternalistic compulsion. However, this would not be convincing as it is not hard to find empirical evidence to the contrary. For example the day after the wearing of safety belts in cars was made compulsory, the news media featured a man whose car had overturned. It was, he said, the first time he had ever worn a safety belt, he would not have done so but for the law, and without it he would almost certainly have died or been seriously injured. Naturally he was delighted that the law had compelled him in his own interest, and I am sure that he, and everyone else whose lives have been saved by that law, feel that being deprived of a little freedom, and perhaps even a little self-respect, is a small price to pay for the benefit of being alive.

Yet even if people do not always know what is good for them and paternalism sometimes makes them happier, we are still uneasy about compelling people in their own interest. Paternalism seems to fit badly with our ideas of equality and liberty and we are wary of it. I think part of our mistrust of paternalism is that we are aware of the dangers of allowing people to use power over others on grounds that are hard to define and for reasons which owe much to subjective value judgments. It is not easy in practice to distinguish between what A knows will make B happier, what A thinks will make B happier and what A believes ought to make B happier, and there is also the danger that A may use a general acceptance of paternalism to do things which he says are for the benefit of B but are really in his own interests. Then again, if we acknowledge that individuals may be mistaken as to which is the best course of action to pursue (and this human fallibility is part of the rationale of paternalism) then we must accept that this may be true of the paternalist as well. It is not only B who may be ignorant, under stress or subject to illegitimate persuasion: this may also be true of A. There are no experts in living to whom we would hand over the running of our lives, as we might entrust our car to a mechanic or our appendix to a surgeon. To acknowledge that there may be difficulties in distinguishing genuine paternalism from its counterfeit is not, of course, to show that there is anything wrong with paternalism. To say that A may be mistaken, hypocritical or corrupt does not tell us what, if anything, would be wrong with his actions if they were prompted by a sincere wish to help B and a correct assessment of what is in B's interests. Paternalism is a use of power over other people and so it is understandable that we should be worried about its potential misuse. However, although some of our suspicion of paternalism comes from the fear that the power of the paternalist may be misused, there is also some doubt as to whether even genuine concern for the best interests of others is a sufficient justification for compelling them to do what we and not they have chosen.

There appear to be two different and conflicting sets of ideas and no clear way of resolving the conflict between them. On the one hand is the belief that there is something of value for individuals in making their own choices, simply because they are their own, and that for these always to be made by someone else, no matter how wise, would be in some way demeaning. Together with this goes the knowledge that, as a matter of fact, we learn to make wise decisions by sometimes making foolish ones, and so, if we are ever going to learn we must have the opportunity to make our own mistakes. On the other hand, most people, even Mill, believe that there are some circumstances in which we are justified in coercing people for their own good, and that anyone who is concerned about the welfare of others should not always stand by and watch them come to some predictable and preventable harm. What appears to be needed and what many have attempted to formulate is a principle or set of principles which lay down the conditions under which paternalism is justified, thus enabling us to secure the benefits of allowing some limited paternalism and to avoid or minimise its dangers. (That paternalism should be *limited* appears not to be in doubt. I have not encountered one claim that we are always justified in coercing people according to our ideas of what is good for them.)

Mill's principle is that:

> Despotism is a legitimate mode of government in dealing with barbarians, provided the end be their improvement and the means justified by actually achieving that end.[5]

In practice it is not as unproblematic as Mill suggests to know what counts as an 'improvement' (or, indeed, who should call someone else a barbarian!) but the principle for justifying paternalism is clear. Other suggestions are that paternalism is justified if

1) there is no alternative way of achieving the same end
2) there is good reason to believe that the person coerced would or will consent to the paternalistic interference
3) the coerced person is helped to realise his or her own ends
4) the judgment or desire which is overruled has been clouded in some relevant way, such as by ignorance, irrationality, emotional stress, inexperience or some other such cause
5) the harm to be avoided is serious

6) the paternalism restricts present freedom but enlarges the possibility of future choice
7) the value of what would have been chosen is not great

It is necessary to consider these suggestions in some detail to see if any of them provides a justification of paternalism.

Paternalism and the Chance of Success

The requirements that paternalism should firstly be effective and secondly be the only effective way of achieving the same end may seem inappropriate criteria in a consideration of whether paternalism is justified because they refer to the practical questions of whether it works and whether it works better than anything else. However I believe they are important, for the question of whether paternalism works (i.e. does secure advantages for the coerced person) is not merely empirical and therefore irrelevant to a judgment of whether it is justified. The aim of paternalism is to benefit the person who is coerced and if the result of A's paternalism is disastrous for B (and if any sensible person could have guessed that it would be) then the cry 'I only meant it for the best' will not serve as a justification. The question of whether there is an alternative way of achieving the same end is also relevant because if we admit that there are disadvantages in coercing people we must consider whether we could secure the advantages of paternalism another way. Dworkin considers this to be sufficiently important to make it one of his two principles of justified paternalism, saying that if there is another way of accomplishing the same end we should use it no matter how expensive it may be.[6]

Paternalism: the Only Way

As there are practical disadvantages to paternalistic coercion as well as moral scruples about its use, it is clearly preferable to use other methods of benefiting the object of paternalism if this is possible. However, Dworkin's principle that other ways should be used regardless of expense is too strong. A point will surely be reached at which the expense of an alternative method is sufficiently high to make it prohibitive. For example, a government which wanted drivers to wear safety belts would, following Dworkin's principle, have to be prepared to conduct personal interviews with every driver individually, pointing out the dangers, explaining the evidence and trying to convince the drivers of the wisdom of wearing their belts before they could bring in paternalistic legislation. If the powers of persuasion of junior civil servants were not successful, then presumably the Ministers of Transport and Health would have to try before coercion could legitimately be used. The possibility that the time and money involved could be spent more profitably, and that it ought to be, cannot be ruled out — as it would be by Dworkin's principle.

Paternalism and Consent

As paternalism is concerned with making people do what they have not chosen to do, first thoughts would suggest that paternalism and consent have little to do with each other. However Dworkin argues that 'the basic notion of consent is important and seems to me the only acceptable way of trying to delimit an area of justified paternalism.'[7] To overcome the apparent incompatibility Dworkin stretches the notion of consent so that it contains prior and retrospective consent to specific instances of paternalism, consent to a government which may make paternalistic laws, and consent to general aims which may require paternalism for their achievement. His example of Odysseus, begging in advance to have his eyes and ears stopped even if later he says he has changed his mind, shows prior consent clearly, but it illustrates what is a minority of cases of paternalism, for we do not usually ask in advance for specific future restrictions. On the other hand we quite frequently look back and say we are glad we were made to learn French or wear a safety belt, even though we did not wish to at the time, because we now appreciate the benefits. However, though we may subsequently approve of previous coercion we cannot consent to it, for consent precludes coercion: and even if we do give subsequent approval the presence of this forgiveness or gratitude for previous coercion does not necessarily mean that the paternalism was justified.

Firstly, it is possible that, although the person who was compelled subsequently approves of the compulsion, the beneficial results might have been achieved by other, non-coercive, methods. Secondly, and more importantly I believe, the person who gives the retrospective consent may have been so changed by the coercion that they are not able to do anything but consent, because the restriction and compulsion were geared to obtaining subsequent consent and, if successful, will have created a person who is incapable of refusing that consent. For example, people who have been brainwashed or indoctrinated may say and even believe that their coercion was a justifiable method of introducing them to 'the truth'. However they cannot consent to it for they do not have the alternative of not approving. Even in less extreme cases we may subsequently approve of coercion that was either unnecessary or predominantly harmful.

Human beings are resilient and often manage to extract something of value, or what they think is of value, from the most unlikely or unpleasant experiences, but it does not follow that a paternalist would be justified in creating these circumstances in order to produce that 'something of value'. The six of the best which 'made me what I am' may have done just that, and have gained subsequent approval, but it may have left the subject unable to appreciate that its main effect has been destructive rather than beneficial. I would argue that when we are considering paternalism, the likelihood that the person to be coerced will later approve of their coercion is an important factor in the decision of whether the paternalism is justified, but the probability, or even the certainty, of retrospective consent is not sufficient to justify coercion.

Imposing a Conception of the 'Good'

Indoctrinators and brain-washers restrict and coerce in order to impose their own conception of the good on their victims. It might be thought, therefore, that it is this imposition of values which is wrong and that compulsion which assists those who are compelled to achieve their ends would be justified. I do not believe, however, that 'helpful' paternalism is always justified, nor that imposing a conception of the good is always wrong. My daughter occasionally asked me to 'make' her do some music practice when an exam was in the offing because she feared that without a little coercion she would not do enough. Usually I agreed, and the coercion needed to help her achieve her conception of the good (passing the exam) was minimal. If it had been greater, however, I might rightly have refused to turn the house into a battlefield and myself into a tyrant to help her achieve her ends, particularly if I believed her long-term interests would have been better served if I had imposed my conception of the good, which involves learning the value of self-motivation and self-discipline.

Some of the situations in which we might most readily agree that paternalism is justified are those in which the paternalist's conception of the good is imposed: when dealing with the very young, the suicidal or the mentally ill, for example. We may make the assumption that those we coerce will come to appreciate our compulsion when they are older or less disturbed, but we are not helping them achieve the ends they have acknowledged. It is because we believe they are mistaken in their values that we judge them to be in need of paternalism. Odysseus did not want to hear the sirens, and made his wishes known in advance, so when he was coerced he was compelled to do what he really wanted. Usually, however, we do not have a convenient statement about what others want to achieve, nor their permission to coerce them for their own good, and so we have to make assumptions about what they will want, or would want if they were fully rational and aware of all the facts. It is when we do this, that we run the risk of being mistaken. Some of our assumptions, of course, are quite reasonable. We rightly assume that people do not want to cut their faces on their car windscreens and most people accept a paternalistic law insisting we wear seat belts. This law restricts our freedom, but it does so to help us achieve our own ends and in accordance with our own wishes — the wish not to be thrown through the windscreen. If we stop someone committing suicide, however, we are not helping them to achieve their own ends and are imposing our own conception of the good — continued life — on them.

Paternalism, Ignorance and Irrationality

There is always the possibility of a mistake when we assume we know what other people want, but the difficulty is compounded when we try to imagine what they would want (if they were not irrational or ignorant) or what they ought to want. Even if it were possible to be certain of what the rational thing to do would be on every occasion, there would be little individual freedom if the wise and knowledgeable were always justified in coercing the ignorant and foolish. As it is there are no experts whose views on what it is rational to desire should be followed, for individuals and individual tastes vary.

In an attempt to overcome the problem of choices which might appear to be irrational but are genuine wishes and individual preferences, John Hodson makes a distinction between unencumbered and rational decisions.[8] An unencumbered decision is not the same as the choice of a fully rational person: it is the decision of an individual, but unencumbered by such factors as ignorance, emotional stress, undue influence or mental illness. The advantage of this distinction is that it places emphasis on the choices of individuals rather than on a fixed view of what any and every rational person would want. Thus we could accept as unencumbered the decision of a mountaineer who claimed not to want to die to make a hazardous ascent. An unencumbered decision is an individual's personal decision, and individuals vary in what they want and think important.

However, I think the notion of unencumbered decisions is less useful than it first appears, because the value judgment on what it is rational to want is simply replaced by another value judgment on whether the decision is encumbered. On one level it is simple and straightforward to see if ignorance has encumbered a decision. For example, if you do not know that smoking is dangerous then your decision to smoke is encumbered. However, in other circumstances the judgment that ignorance has encumbered a decision will be influenced by the values of the person making the judgment. I know I am not alone in feeling that if those who disagree with me knew what I know they would come to think as I do on the disputed subject. It can only be their ignorance or perhaps the undue influence of others which prevents them from seeing things as I do! How natural, then, for a powerful would-be paternalist to take any disagreement as a sign that judgments have been encumbered, and to overrule them. Also, if a decision is wrong then it must be encumbered, by ignorance, false reasoning or both. As none of us has perfect knowledge, all of our judgments are encumbered to some extent, and so it cannot be a sufficient condition of justified paternalism that the judgment or choice that is overruled was encumbered in some way.

Paternalism and the Avoidance of Serious Harm

So far, in my attempt to discover when paternalism is justified, I have been concerned mainly with certain features of the person whose freedom is to be restricted, such as whether they consent to the restriction or are incapable of making rational decisions. However, it is possible that the justification for paternalism lies not in something about the person whose freedom is restricted but in the nature of the act which is forbidden or prevented, and it is to this suggestion that I now turn, considering first whether it is the seriousness of possible harm that justifies paternalistic intervention. It might be questioned whether the size of the disaster to be averted should make any difference when a principle is at stake, for we do not say that people ought to keep big promises and not tell big lies but that little ones do not matter. However, I believe that in the case of paternalism it is relevant for unlike, perhaps, truth telling or promise keeping, paternalism is never desirable as such, but merely sometimes better than the alternatives: we never celebrate it, but see only if we can excuse it. A decision on when paternalism is more desirable than the alternatives must be influenced, then, by what the alternatives are, and so the question of whether the intervention will prevent serious harm or a minor mistake is relevant to its justification.

Mill was right to say that our own decisions have a special value simply because they are our own, regardless of the content of the decision. The taking of decisions which affect us is inextricably linked with our self-esteem and so any overruling of our personal decisions has to be for important reasons. However, for most people, injury, death and financial ruin are serious misfortunes to be avoided (or in the case of death, postponed) when possible, so if we have to weigh the value of a life against the more nebulous notion of the self-esteem which comes from making our own decisions, we usually decide in favour of the life — not least because when that has gone the self-esteem and possibility of making other decisions have gone also. The calculation would be different if instead of saving life we were preventing a small blunder or minor inconvenience.

Paternalism and the Increase of Future Freedom

It might be noted at this point that the various factors to be considered in a decision of whether paternalism is justified are not entirely separate. The possibility of death or serious injury, for example, would be regarded by most people as a misfortune and so any paternalistic intervention which prevented it would assist the coerced person to achieve their own ends and would probably receive retrospective approval. The seriousness of the harm to be avoided is related also to the criterion of enlarging or enhancing future freedom, which Dworkin considers to be very important to a justification of paternalism.[9] Certainly people who are alive, healthy and well-informed will have a wider opportunity for future choice than the dead, injured or ignorant, and so present restrictions which preserve life or promote health and knowledge may make for greater future freedom. However, the increase of future freedom cannot be a sufficient condition for justified paternalism or we would be compelled constantly to keep our options open. There are many things we do which produce irreversible changes in our lives and restrict our future freedom: we take and give up jobs, get married and have children, and these cannot be delayed indefinitely for the sake of enlarged future choice. Making decisions and accepting the inevitable consequences are part of what it is to live a rational and responsible life. It cannot be that preventing people from making decisions now that would close options for them in the future is always justified, for the consequences of choices made now will inevitably influence and restrict the possibility of making different choices later.

The Subjective Value of What Has to Be Given Up

The final factor which I mentioned as relevant to a decision about the justification of paternalism does not refer exclusively to the act which is enforced or forbidden or to the person whose choice is overruled or prevented. It is the consideration of the value to the person who is coerced of what s/he is forced to give up. Firstly, of course, the person has to forgo making an autonomous choice, but secondly s/he has to give up whatever that choice would have been. If it is believed that freedom of choice itself is the crucial issue then the second consideration — the value of what would have been chosen — need not concern us at all. If it is the choosing that is all-important and not what is chosen, then choosing a brand of washing powder is as important as choosing a government, and being forbidden to watch *Driller Killer* as important as being prevented from hearing that the local beach is contaminated with radio-active waste. It is because this is not the case, that the value of what would have been chosen is relevant to a decision of whether paternalism is justified.

If we assume that motor cyclists do not usually want to die then we might agree with a law enforcing the wearing of crash helmets. For most riders this would involve only minor inconvenience and the cost of the helmet, but for motor cyclists who are also Sikhs it also involves disregarding a requirement of their religion. The benefit would be the same but the value of what has to be given up would be much greater. Similarly a law requiring the wearing of safety belts is intended to save lives, and a law forbidding hang gliding, mountaineering or pot-holing might have the same intention. However, while the first law would necessitate only installing safety belts and remembering to use them, the second law would entail adventurous spirits having to give up one of their great pleasures in life. The benefit of increased safety might be the same, but the value of what had to be given up would be much greater. However, it is not the case that paternalism is justified as long as the people whose freedom is restricted do not have to give up anything they value greatly. Once again I would argue that this *relevant* factor is not a deciding factor, and, like the other considerations mentioned so far, neither a necessary nor sufficient condition for justified paternalism.

The Paternalist

In this attempt to find a principle of justified paternalism I have considered some features of the person whose freedom is restricted and also the nature of the act which is forbidden. I have not yet looked at the paternalist, except to say that we are rightly wary of powerful people who claim to know what is good for others and to have the right to enforce their views. The very word 'paternalist' conjures up a picture of an interfering busybody like Lady Catherine De Burgh who:

> whenever any of the cottagers were disposed to be quarrelsome, dis-
> contented or too poor . . . sallied forth into the village to settle their
> differences, silence their complaints and scold them into harmony and
> plenty.[10]

It is clear that Lady Catherine enjoys managing other people's affairs, and one cannot imagine her worrying about the morality of her interference, or thinking that the cottagers' wishes, plans and purposes were as important to them as hers were to her, and as worthy of consideration. In short, paternalists of her type do not regard the objects of their paternalism as persons to be respected, and I suggest that respect for persons is essential to a justification of paternalism.

Paternalism and Respect for Persons

By this I do not mean that it is a separate criterion — number eight on my list — which we look for and assess in the same way as the others. It underlies these criteria and they are ways in which it may be expressed. For example, if we respect someone as a person but believe that circumstances are such that we should overrule their wishes in their own interest, we would want to feel that they would eventually consent to our action, but could not engineer this consent by destroying their ability to withhold it. Similarly we would want to enlarge their future prospects rather than restrict them and, respecting their aims and desires, only *in extremis* would we impose our ends on them. Aware of the dangers of paternalism, and the value of autonomous decisions we would seek to persuade and convince if this were possible, and only resort to paternalism if there seemed no other reasonable way of benefiting the object of our paternalism.

Respect for persons excludes the possibility of condescension, tyranny or using people as means to an end they do not share. It provides the basis of a paternalism based on fundamental equality, though clearly in one sense paternalism does not belong in a relationship between equals. Within the relationship one person is, perhaps, far-sighted, experienced and powerful while the other is not, but that does not alter the fact that the paternalist should see the other as a person with plans, wishes and ends of their own, and a right to freedom as great as that of the paternalist. However, as was argued in Chapter 4, we do not have an absolute right to freedom, and we do have obligations and responsibilities towards other members of the community. Sometimes a conflict may arise between our responsibility for the welfare of others and our obligation to respect their freedom, but when those others are young and/or ignorant, irrational or in danger I believe our responsibility for their welfare will sometimes have to extend to overruling their wishes. It will never extend to considering those wishes unimportant or irrelevant.

Conclusion

There are no absolute criteria by which we can judge when paternalistic acts are justified, and no definitive list of the paternalistic behaviour and attitudes consistent with respecting persons. We can only try to balance the value to individuals of making an autonomous choice; the seriousness of the harm from which we seek to protect them; the likelihood of their subsequent consent to our compulsion; the value to them of what must be given up and the acceptability (or otherwise) of alternatives; the state of mind of the person whose decision is to be overruled; the possibility of protecting them or promoting their welfare by non-coercive means; the possibility that we may be wrong in our assessment of their interests, and then make our decision. If we are sincere in our belief that we are justified in our action, then we should be prepared for others to act in a similar way to protect us and promote our welfare also.

Notes and References

1 J. S. Mill, *On Liberty* p.78
2 Ibid p.78
3 H. L. A. Hart, *Law, Liberty and Morality* p.32–3
4 Ibid.
5 Mill, op. cit. p.78
6 Gerald Dworkin, 'Paternalism.' in Laslett and Fishkin *Philosophy, Politics and Society* 5th Series. p.96
7 Ibid p.89
8 John D. Hodson, 'The Principle of Paternalism.' in *American Philosophical Quarterly* 14
9 Dworkin, op. cit.
10 Jane Austen, *Pride and Prejudice*

Chapter 7

Paternalism Towards Children

In the last chapter I claimed that paternalism can be justified by reference to two notions — responsibility for the welfare of other members of the community and respect for persons. I argued that we could have no right to intervene in other people's personal decisions unless it were the case that we have some responsibility for their welfare, and although the existence of this responsibility could not be proved the consequences of assuming that it did not exist would generally be found unacceptable. At the same time I accepted that condoning the use of power by individuals or groups over others less powerful than themselves was potentially dangerous, and might reinforce inequalities of power and freedom. I argued that for the paternalism to be justified it must not only have been in the interests of the coerced but that the paternalist must respect the persons who were coerced as individuals with purposes of their own and as equals in importance if not in knowledge or experience. I said that there were no absolute criteria by which we could judge when paternalism was justified and no definitive list of the paternalistic behaviour consistent with respecting persons. However, I claimed that there were certain factors (such as the likelihood of subsequent consent, ignorance or lack of understanding of unperceived danger etc.) the presence of which would support a claim that paternalism was justified in a particular instance.

I now wish to argue that paternalism towards children can be justified in the same way and with reference to the same notions of responsibility for the welfare of others and respect for persons. It would not be necessary to make this point if it were not widely assumed that paternalism towards adults and children are very different activities — the former rarely if ever justified: the latter self-evidently so. Although those who are antipathetic to paternalism towards adults sometimes make an effort to explain why their principles should not apply to all, more frequently they assume that the basis for the

74

difference in treatment is so obvious and unproblematic that it needs no explanation. The particular problem of paternalism for children is either ignored or else dismissed in a brief aside in which the author points out that what has been argued applies only to adults. When I say that paternalism for children is a particular problem I mean, of course, that it is and should be recognized as a particular problem for those who claim paternalism is right for children but not for adults, for they have to justify treating the two groups differently. I believe however, that children are part of the general problem of paternalism, not a separate species of sub-persons or possessions to whom the adult ideals of freedom and self-respect do not apply.

Mill's 'Mature Faculties'

Often, as I have said, the difference between children and adults which is taken to make paternalism right for one and not the other is assumed to be so obvious that it is not stated, let alone examined, but when reasons for differential treatment are given they are usually that children lack some adult competence. Mill, for example makes it clear that his antipaternalist principle is:

> meant to apply to human beings in the maturity of their faculties . . . (and not) children or . . . young persons below the age which the law may fix as that of manhood or womanhood,[1]

and says this is because:

> those who are still in a state to require being taken care of by others must be protected against their own actions as well as against external injury.[2]

He assumes that the difference between adults and children is important enough and clear enough to make it justifiable to protect children but not adults against their own actions, and the difference of which he speaks is that adults have mature faculties and can take care of themselves while children cannot. Now whether we agree about that or not, once the qualities of maturity and self-sufficiency have been isolated as the criteria by which we judge whether someone should be free from paternalism or not, then we should ensure that any children who show these qualities should not be subject to paternalism and any immature dependent adults should.

It is true that we associate 'maturity' with adults, but whatever 'mature faculties' are they are not acquired simply by reaching the age of twenty-one or eighteen. 'Maturity' encompasses, amongst other things, the ideas of rationality, experience, steadiness and consistency of purpose and ability to see and plan ahead, all of which we would hope to gain with age, but unfortunately do not always do so: and if we do gain them, we do not do so in the way we gain grey hair and wrinkles, merely by staying alive long enough. As Mill himself points out 'the mental and the moral, like the muscular powers are improved only by being used'[3] and presumably this is as true for children as it is for adults. No-one could seriously claim that clear judgment, common sense, rationality, knowledge, experience and a sense of purpose descend on people on their twenty-first or eighteenth birthdays, or even that they finally spring into flower at that time fully operational at last after years of gradual development. Anyone, if pressed, would have to admit that some children are more rational, knowledgeable and purposeful than some adults. What follows, then, is that if it is on the basis of ignorance, irrationality and inexperience that we decide whether a person needs paternalistic treatment we cannot maintain a rigid distinction between adults and children in this matter.

The Tluda and the Dlihc

It would be wrong to suggest that all who believe paternalism for adults is not justified are unaware of any contradictions in their position. Francis Schrag, for example, examines the common intuition that paternalism is justified for children and not adults and tries to explain the inconsistency. In an attempt to make us aware of our unexamined assumptions about the rightness of paternalism for children and its wrongness for adults, Schrag invents a society called the Namuh. In this society the strong intelligent knowledgeable Tluda control the weak ignorant Dlihc, meting out arbitrary punishments and, though claiming to love them and be concerned for their welfare, restricting their freedom. He says 'Any such hierarchically ordered society would be universally condemned by almost every writer on ethics since Kant.'[4] Yet this (with the names reversed) is our society.

Schrag is very clear about the difficulties of our society's attitude to paternalism. He considers whether children, as a group, are different to adults, as a group, in ways which are relevant to their different treatment. He takes all the differences which are usually suggested, plus a few more, considers them as criteria for the justification of paternalism for children and finds them all un-satisfactory. If we take linguistic competence as the difference between children and adults, then the age of change-over is nearer six than eighteen; if the differ-ence is sexual maturity, then the change comes in the early teens; if it is the attainment of some intellectual standard (perhaps Piaget's formal operations) then some children will qualify early and some adults not at all. If ability to maintain oneself were taken to be the relevant characteristic, then some children would be quite capable of doing this, whereas some people with dis-abilities would not and would, therefore, be legitimate targets for paternalism. Schrag claims this would be unacceptable, however, because although adults with disabilities may require assistance this does not entail that they need to be coerced in their own interests. Finally, he argues, if we try to justify pater-nalism on the utilitarian grounds that it will make children happier, then we must still explain why this would not justify paternalism for adults also.

What Schrag wants, but cannot find, is a rationale for paternalism that will confirm our present beliefs and arrangements. He wants to find a dis-tinction between children and adults that will justify paternalism for the former and not the latter, and he cannot find it, but instead of concluding that paternalism is, in principle as acceptable or unacceptable for children as it is for adults and for the same reasons, he comes out in favour of a distinction he has shown to be insecurely based. Schrag says we have to choose between two views — either that there is a clear distinction between children and adults or that there is not. Having shown that there is not, he then opts for the view that there is, because, he claims, this is essential if we are to maintain that paternalism for adults is wrong. The second, gradualist, view contains the danger of justifying paternalism for adults and so we must avoid it. Schrag shows a position to be untenable and then chooses to hold it for no other reason than that he dislikes the implication of the alternative. He says:

> Perhaps some will consider this decision to support a kind of 'noble lie', but if so it is not one in which a few deceive the masses for their own good, but rather one in which we all believe for our own good.[5]

Leaving aside the fact that many children do not believe it, (but perhaps Schrag does not consider them part of 'us all'), it is still not a 'noble lie'. It is a con-venient belief, untenable when examined, which enables adults to maintain their fantasies of self-sufficiency, their power and their assumption of superiority over the younger members of society.

Another attempt to justify different attitudes to paternalism towards children and paternalism toward adults is made by Geoffrey Scarre. Scarre claims that Schrag's mistake is in looking for a rationale which allows some paternalism for children and none at all for adults, whereas:

> a fair criterion of justified paternalism will refer to some feature or features of persons which will in principle be capable of being possessed by both children and adults, though it will in practice be possessed by far more of the former than the latter.[6]

He claims that Schrag overemphasizes the importance of liberty for adults and therefore is unwilling to let anything count as a justification for paternalism for them. In this, Scarre is surely correct, as he is in his identification of what would constitute a fair criterion of justified paternalism. Where he is wrong, I suggest, is in identifying certain human characteristics — those which he says render paternalism unjustified — as adult characteristics, when in fact they are possessed by children as well.

The Difference Between Adults and Children

Scarre says:

> children are inexperienced in the ways of the world and are incapable of forming life-plans or systematic purposes; indeed the capacity to form coherent purposes and the development of the will-power to stick by them are part of what distinguishes adults from children.[7]

However, inexperience of the ways of the world is a vague expression and too inexact a concept for us to base a justification of paternalism on it. Unarguably children have not been around for as long as adults and so are likely to be relatively inexperienced compared with adults, but a person of twenty-five is likely to be relatively inexperienced compared with a person of sixty. Relative lack of experience cannot justify paternalism, then, or it would be justified for all but the elderly. It is true that we gain experience as we grow older but we do not do so uniformly, and as a teacher of young children I am frequently surprised at what does and what does not fall within their experience. Some children, at quite a young age, have met and coped successfully with situations that I did not encounter until years later — if at all. Certainly, inexperience of particular circumstances is a factor which should be taken into account when paternalism is considered. A child with no experience of the dangers of tides and off-shore winds, for example, should not be let loose on a windy sea on a lilo. However, that is an example of particular inexperience justifying a particular instance of paternalism. It is not the case that children's inexperience justifies generalized paternalism towards them. If children have not the experience or understanding to cope with traffic or electricity then they need to be protected from them; if they are inexperienced in managing money or making decisions about their school work then they will need help, but, as was stressed in the chapter on children's rights, they are not a separate class of beings who are always in need of adult direction and subject to adult authority. Inexperience is a handicap to be overcome and adults' responsibility towards children is not only to protect them from the consequences of their inexperience, but also to help them gain the important experience they need.

Despite the admitted relative inexperience of the young, I do not think Scarre is right to say they are unable to form life-plans and systematic purposes. Some children decide when quite young what job they want to do when they grow up, and work steadily towards the realization of their ambition. Many children, when they do have a chance to plan and control some area of their lives, do it carefully and sensibly: not always, of course, but then nor do we. If children have no life-plans and systematic purposes then those adults responsible for their welfare will, until that situation changes, have the duty to make such plans for them that will keep their options open. They will also have the duty to help bring about change, so that the children are able to form their own plans.

Another characteristic which Scarre takes to be the prerogative of adults is love of freedom. He rejects Schrag's analogy of the Tluda and Dlihc because he says it misleads us into thinking of the downtrodden Dlihc as possessing our own adult love of freedom, whereas really they are children and therefore quite different. Scarre gives what he takes to be an example of this difference when he says that we cannot force an adult alcoholic to dry out because this would be imposing our plans on him in place of his own and would thus be an insult. However, he says:

children do not have systems of purposes of their own, so it does not infringe their rights to intervene on their behalf when their irrationality threatens their well-being.[8]

This is not an explanation of why paternalism is justified for children but a set of assertions about their nature which he does not back up, and with which I disagree strongly. Observation of children's behaviour suggests that they often do have systems of purposes of their own and are affronted by the restriction of their freedom by powerful adults. According to Scarre's view an eleven year-old child may want to be a doctor or gymnast and may work systematically towards that end for years, but may justifiably be coerced because 'children do not have systems of purposes of their own.' Adult alcoholics, on the other hand, may drift aimlessly doing whatever may be counterproductive to their stated aims, yet they may not justifiably be coerced because they are adult and adults are insulted and their rights infringed if we impose our plans on them. I wonder how these propositions might be falsified. What would a child or an adult have to do to destroy Scarre's belief that the latter has coherent purposes and will-power and the former has not?

Empirical evidence (and memory) also seem to show that children do share the adult's love of freedom. There can be few children who read *Swallows and Amazons* without envying the Walkers their anti-paternalist father. His telegram 'BETTER DROWNED THAN DUFFERS IF NOT DUFFERS WON'T DROWN'[9] does not appeal to me now as a parent. I would prefer living duffers any day, but as a child I thought it a wonderful sentiment. Children's books are full of children whose parents are conveniently dead, missing, absent-minded or amazingly understanding in allowing their children the freedom to follow up the exciting possibilities that present themselves, and the fact that these are so popular would suggest that, in their fantasies at least, children value the freedom to do things for themselves without parental interference. In fact as well as in fiction, children have purposes and plans of their own, want very much to be able to carry them out and are sometimes affronted by adult power over them. It is because we have already decided that we will treat them as if this were not so that we dismiss their plans, their desires, their dignity and sense of worth as individuals as less important than our own, and we set up a false distinction between us, the adults, who value freedom and whose plans and purposes must be respected, and children who do not share those feelings.

Paternalism is always something of an affront: it is so from the first time we try to assert our own wishes as infants (and, for our own good, are not allowed to succeed) until the day we die in the nice safe Home we are moved to because our own home is deemed to be unsuitable. We should admit that and then argue that it is sometimes better to insult, affront or impose our will on others (adults and children) than let them be killed, cheated or exploited. Paternalism is not ideal: it is always second best to autonomy. We would much rather explain to young children why it is not a good idea for them to put their fingers into an electric socket, and we would prefer that walking across the park at night was so safe that we did not have to forbid young teenagers to do it, but we cannot organize all the circumstances of our lives so that paternalism is never necessary — either for children or adults. When paternalism for children is necessary and right it is so not because children's hurt feelings, individual wishes or self-respect are somehow less real or less important than those of adults, but for the same reasons that it is sometimes justified for adults. The same factors have to be considered: whether the original decision or desire is rational; made from ignorance or knowledge; will enhance or restrict future freedom; is consistent with other aims (especially valued long-term ends), is likely to result in harm; is considered particularly valuable or important, and whether the paternalism is likely to be approved subsequently, is likely to be successful and is the only practicable way of achieving its object. Paternalism for children is justified (when it *is* justified) on the same grounds as for adults — that they are unique persons with purposes and plans of their own and whose individuality we value, but for whose welfare we have some responsibility so that we cannot stand idly by and watch them come to harm.

Notes and References

1. J.S. Mill, *On Liberty* p. 78
2. Ibid p. 78
3. Ibid p. 126
4. Francis Schrag, 'The Child in the Moral Order'. *Philosophy* 52 p. 117–24
5. Ibid.
6. Geoffrey Scarre, 'Children and Paternalism' *Philosophy* 55 p. 121
7. Ibid p. 119–20
8. Ibid p. 123
9. Arthur Ransome, *Swallows and Amazons* p. 15

Chapter 8

Compulsory Education and the Freedom of Children

Having looked at some of the questions and problems about liberty and restricting liberty, about adults' freedom and children's freedom, I want to focus more specifically now on the implications of my arguments for the upbringing and education of our children today. I want to consider something of what it would mean to us as parents, teachers, citizens, politicians and planners if we were to take children and their freedom seriously, and include them as part of 'us'. Particularly, I shall consider the sort of education we would give our children if we lived up to our own rhetoric about freedom and democracy. As perhaps the first question about education that would arise, if children's freedom were sincerely valued, is whether education and/or schooling should be compulsory, I will start with this subject, and consider whether compulsory education is a morally justifiable restriction of children's freedom on paternalistic, or any other grounds.

As I have claimed throughout this book, freedom is not an indivisible entity. There are many freedoms, some of which are more valuable than others and many of which are incompatible: the restriction of some freedoms can lead to an increase of freedom in other areas, and the restriction of the freedom of one person or group can lead to greater freedom for others. The important questions about compulsory education for me, then, concern whose freedoms and which freedoms are restricted, whether these are important and valued freedoms, whether their loss is compensated for by a gain in more valuable freedoms or other goods, and whether the restriction is justified. However, as it has been denied that compulsory education is a restriction of freedom at all, perhaps it is necessary to clear that out of the way before going on to the questions I consider more important and interesting.

Does Compulsory Education Restrict Freedom?[1]

The view that compulsory education restricts freedom has been challenged on the grounds that most people would do what is required by law anyway, and so the law does not affect their behaviour. This view is put by M.S. Katz, who objects to the use of words 'compulsion' and 'coercion' in the context of school attendance laws.[2] He claims these are not coercive because most people do not obey them simply through fear of the consequences of disobedience, and that 'Compulsory school attendance laws codify an existing norm or standard'.[3] It is true that if we were planning to do anyway what the law says we must we do not *feel* coerced or oppressed, but laws which close certain options to us do restrict our freedom even if we have no wish to choose what is forbidden, or even if we are unaware of its existence. Katz also claims that to speak of the laws as forms of compulsion or coercion is to 'de-emphasize' their legitimacy, but this is to fall into the trap of thinking that, as he disapproves of coercion and approves of both freedom and compulsory school attendance, the school attendance laws cannot be coercive.[4] Put simplistically the argument is the common one that freedom is good, restriction is bad, so whenever we have a case of what appears to be a necessary or desirable restriction, then either the freedom is not really freedom or the restriction is not really a restriction. However, it is not the legitimacy or otherwise of a restriction, nor our approval or disapproval of it that makes it restrictive of freedom. Not all freedoms are desirable and not all restrictions are evil, and though there is a need to justify restrictions there is no need to explain them away or disguise them as something else. Laws can compel and coerce and still be legitimate.

Does Compulsory Education Restrict *Children's Freedom?*

It has been suggested that although laws compel they do not restrict children's freedom because children lack the capacity for freedom. Freedom, according to this view, is something we achieve when we have certain abilities and as children lack those abilities and cannot achieve freedom they cannot be deprived of it. Locke has been accused of holding this view by Peter Gardner[5] who quotes him as saying that man's freedom is 'grounded in his reason' and that to 'turn him loose . . . before he has reason to guide him is not allowing him . . . to be free.[6] This suggests that reason is necessary for freedom and that without reason there can be no liberty. Gardner criticizes this thesis, not on the grounds that children do have reason but because:

> the amoral, the untutored, those with under-developed physiques and intellects and those whose powers have not been liberated for the common good, can be free from many constraints and impediments and free to do many things.[7]

Freedom, he says, is not something we achieve.

Gardner is right to draw attention to the basic freedom of not being pushed around, a freedom which all who are reasonably aware of what is happening to them may enjoy, but mistaken to assume that this is the only, or only important, freedom. Exercising freedom (as opposed to simply not being coerced) implies choosing between alternatives, and in order to choose we must have an idea of what appears to us to be a good, some knowledge of relevant facts, and the ability to reason. Without these we do not choose between alternatives, but merely drift or plump for one course of action rather than another. However, as has been stressed previously, there are many different freedoms. It is mistaken to claim that, as rational thought is required for the exercise of free choice, we are free only when rationally choosing: and it is equally mistaken to deny that the exercise of some freedoms requires rationality and knowledge of desired ends and of means. Not all of the many different freedoms are compatible, and it is possible to be deprived of freedom in one area and thereby enjoy it in another. This, I suggest, is what Locke claimed happens when parents educate their children to become reasonable adults, for what Locke actually said was:

> The freedom of Man and Liberty of acting according to his own Will is grounded on his having Reason . . . To turn him loose to an unrestrain'd Liberty, before he has Reason to guide him, is not allowing him the privilege of his Nature, to be free.[8]

The fuller quotation shows that Locke contrasts two types of freedom: the freedom of acting according to his own will, which depends on having reason, and unrestrained liberty which does not. Locke, then, does accept that children's liberty is restricted in certain ways by their parents, but he believes that a less valuable liberty is given up for a more valuable one.

Is Compulsory Education a Legitimate Restriction of Freedom?

Compulsory education, restricting freedom as it does, is vulnerable to criticism on three different counts: firstly, there is Gardner's criticism that it is a restriction of freedom and all restrictions of freedom are wrong; secondly that though compulsion may be justified in order to achieve certain valuable ends, the ends of compulsory schooling are not valuable; and thirdly, that though the ends may be valuable they are not or cannot be achieved through compulsion.

For those who hold the view that all restrictions of freedom are wrong, to admit that compulsory education restricts freedom is to condemn it. Gardner claims that:

> to a libertarian compulsory education is evil in itself; whatever its benefits he will be under a *prima facie* obligation to do away with it.[9]

This exemplifies the mistaken view that freedom is one thing, always valuable, and that restrictions of freedom are necessarily wrong whatever good may come from them. Gardner holds that 'all restraints are evil in themselves'[10] and yet, inconsistently, he criticizes Dworkin for being prepared to sacrifice justice for freedom.[11] If justice should not be sacrificed for freedom, and it is not always possible to have both, then presumably it is sometimes necessary to restrict freedom to promote justice. Gardner does not explain how a necessary restriction which promotes a valued end such as justice can be evil in itself. Gardner is right to say that 'compulsory education needs justifying precisely because it is compulsory'[12] but he needs to explain how something evil in itself which restricts something valuable in itself can possibly be justified.

Even if one accepts, as most of us do, that it is sometimes right to restrict freedom in order to achieve other valued ends, there will be disagreement about which ends are sufficiently valuable to warrant restrictions and which freedoms are too valuable to be given up. Is the capture of criminals valuable enough to allow the police greater powers to restrict the freedom of those who may be innocent? Is the raising of the living standards of its members sufficiently important for Trade Unions to be allowed to introduce a closed shop? Do the benefits of educating all our children outweigh the loss of liberty that is involved in requiring them to attend school? Such questions of value are very important, not simply so that conclusions can be reached, but because the working out of problems of value is part of our life as members of a community.

The questions of whether the freedom to act according to reason as an adult is incompatible with unrestrained liberty for children, and, if so, which is the more valuable are particularly difficult questions because the unrestrained children, if irrational, cannot judge the value of the education they have not had, while rational adults cannot throw off their rationality and recapture their pre-educated selves. The discussion will not be helped, however, by the insistence that either of these two freedoms is not really a freedom at all. However, as it is necessary to have certain skills and knowledge in order to take part in the debates about which liberties and other goods are more valuable, and these discussions are part of our lives as social beings, we cannot decide in favour of unrestrained liberty for children. Education in a democracy should have as one of its aims that all should be educated to be able to participate fully in their society — to make personal decisions and choices as individuals and to play their part in democratic institutions and decision-making. As Pat White says:

> However much . . . a democratic society values freedom and wishes to allow individuals to pursue their own concerns without interference . . . it cannot refrain from 'interfering' through its appropriate authorities, to ensure that children get an adequate political education.[13]

A Rational Curriculum for Future Freedom

John White also claims that we are justified in restricting children's present freedom for their future benefit, but he emphasizes the value of freedom to choose a way of life as individuals, rather than to participate in joint decision-making. He argues that we cannot know what any person will want to do, or what his conception of the good will be, and so:

> The least harmful course we can follow is to equip him, as far as possible, for the ideal situation — to let him determine himself what the Good shall be for him. To do this we must ensure, (a) that he knows about as many activities or ways of life as possible which he may want to choose for their own sake, and (b) that he is able to reflect on priorities among them from the point of view not only of the present moment but as far as possible of his life as a whole.[14]

In order to approach this ideal situation, and teach what is necessary in the most economical way, White proposes that the curriculum be based on two categories of activities: firstly those which it is necessary to engage in before they can be understood, and secondly, those which may be understood without being engaged in. The first should be taught compulsorily in school, while children should be taught about the second. To put it briefly, in order to be able to choose whether we want to be Mathematicians or not we must be compelled to learn Mathematics, because it is impossible to understand what is involved without doing it. However, the category two activities, which can be understood, so to speak, from the side-lines, should not be part of the compulsory curriculum. All that is necessary is that we should be taught enough *about* them to know whether we would choose to do them.

My first criticism of White's rational curriculum is concerned with learning about category two activities. White rightly says that we can, as adults, understand something of many activities without engaging in them. However, I believe that for young children, at least, the distinction between categories one and two would not be so clear, and that White's curriculum does not seem to be planned to take into account the way they learn. I could certainly tell my infant class that yellow and red paint will make orange, that plants need light, or that the path is twenty metres long; but the information would be meaningless. It is in mixing the colours, comparing the straggly yellow seedlings from the dark cupboard with the healthy green ones from the window ledge, and laying the metre sticks along the path that they come to understand pieces of information that an older person could assimilate through reading or being told. For young children everything is a category one activity.

My second criticism is that even though adults can understand category two activities without engaging in them, White does not show that we can understand enough about them to know why people enjoy them so much. I can know what bird-watching, or chess or scuba diving are without having any idea of their own particular joys and satisfactions, and without that knowledge I am singularly ill-equipped to sit back at the end of my schooling and decide which of those activities will fill my week-ends. If I take to any of them, it is much more likely to be because somebody I know enthuses about them, and I have a go, and gain sufficient pleasure, intrinsic or extrinsic, to want to continue. (There is no need for the pleasure to be intrinsic, or for the activity to be worthwhile 'in its own right'. That it is enjoyed at all is surely a sufficiently good reason to choose to do it.) Again, although adults and older children may be able to *understand* a category two activity without practising it, we may need many years of practice before we can do it properly. If we were to understand an activity first, then decide to do it, and then learn to do it, it might be too late to do it properly. Having a go at skiing at the age of 35 when I understood what it was about and had decided that I would like to try it was very enjoyable, but not nearly such a good way of becoming a competent skier as whizzing around on the slopes from the age of two, like the Austrian children that I met. White's rational curriculum fails to take account of the fact that some skills and activities have to be engaged in from an early age — not so that they may be understood, but so that they can be done properly.

While agreeing that education should prepare children for making choices as adults, and should help them to be informed about the substance of those choices, my main criticism of White's argument is that there is something unrealistic about a curriculum planned to achieve that end alone. White acknowledges that what he calls the ideal situation, of knowing about as many activities and ways of life as possible, and being able to reflect on priorities, is unrealizable, but I would question its desirability as well as its feasibility. Without wanting my life or those of my children to be either irrational or non-rational, I would not want them to be quite as pre-planned and future-orientated as White seems to suggest should be the case. White's model seems to set out life in stages: firstly learning category one activities; learning about category two activities as a preparation for the future; then choosing between them all and choosing a way of life, and then living. My criticism is not that this model neglects the element of chance in life, and the things over which we have no control (White accepts that we cannot have complete autonomy[15]), but that it does not give sufficient value to children's present lives, or to the freedom they have and the choices that they make while they are still children. My children both learned and played the trumpet for years before eventually deciding to give up. Was the only value of all those lessons, practice and Saturday mornings spent in the Brass Group the knowledge that they do not wish to be adult trumpeters? I believe not. If it were, it would be very expensive (of time, money and parental nerves) a way of gaining a small piece of information.

As was argued in the chapter on paternalism, we cannot keep our options open indefinitely for fear of losing opportunities later. The choice to do one thing now will inevitably preclude the possibility of doing something else, and while educationalists and parents must try to ensure that important options are not closed early, they would be as wrong to concentrate exclusively on the future, as the extreme child-centred lobby are to neglect it. Education is necessarily forward looking, and should be about broadening outlook and presenting new possibilities, but to prefer to teach children about a large number of category two activities (perhaps by showing them films) rather than to teach them a smaller number by taking part with a committed enthusiast, is to neglect the importance of an interesting present.

Compulsion and Uniformity

White justifies compulsion in education on the grounds that we are right to restrict children's freedom now in order to increase their autonomy later.[16] There are those, however, who believe that the aim of compulsory education is to create uniformity of opinion and life-style, rather than enable people to make reasoned choices as individuals and a worthwhile contribution to joint decisions, and who criticize it on the grounds that freedom is restricted not for a valued end but for something undesirable. Rothbard, for example, argues that state schools have played a continuing role in suppressing religious dissent and creating uniformity.[17] From Martin Luther to the anti-Catholic Ku-Klux Klan, via various socialists and progressives, supporters of state schooling have wanted to impose a particular and uniform ideology, he claims. Rothbard does not appear to be concerned about the morality of individuals or groups forcing their own children to accept particular beliefs, nor to consider that children may have greater freedom to choose their own values and life-style while attending and after attending a state school than if they were educated according to the beliefs of their parents.

It cannot be denied that compulsory schooling has been used to promote particular ideologies, but what can be denied is that the imposition of ideas and values on children is greater in a society with compulsory education than one without it. Societies cannot avoid passing on ideas to their children, but it is possible to try to teach them to treat ideas critically, and compulsion may be the only way to ensure that all children have the opportunity to do this. Libertarians might be more successful in promoting genuine liberty if they tried to ensure that state schools teach children to adopt a critical attitude to a variety of ideas, rather than risk leaving children to learn nothing but their parents' own beliefs or to be at the mercy of any and every persuasive voice.

Parents' Freedom: Children's Freedom?

Critics of compulsory schooling (and of compulsory education and compulsory state education) can be found amongst those who hold widely differing views about children's freedom. Some are concerned to liberate children from the oppression of school, while the chief or only complaint of others is that it takes away the freedom of parents to decide the content, nature and extent of their children's education. As the law in Britain compels parents to send their children to school (or see that they are educated to an acceptable standard elsewhere) and as it is parents who will eventually be taken to court if they fail to do this, compulsory education is sometimes considered to be a restriction of the freedom of parents rather than children. In fact both are affected, for if the law compels parents to compel their children, then, clearly, children's freedom is restricted, albeit indirectly. However, it should be remembered that most children would not be given the choice of whether or not to go to school even if attendance there were not compulsory. Shakespeare's unwilling schoolboy creeping to his books was no freer to decide whether to go to school than his modern counterpart, despite the difference in law. Unless the law making school attendance compulsory were replaced by one which protected the wishes of children and gave preference to them over those of their parents (as Holt tentatively suggests that it should,[18] then the effective freedom of most children over the decision of whether they should go to school would be no greater without compulsory education than with it.

For some of the most severe critics of compulsory education this would not be seen as a problem, either because they do not value children's freedom or because they do not think about it at all. Both of these attitudes can be found in the essays in Rickenbacker's book *12 Year Sentence*.[19] On the back of this book are eight examples from the United States of the problems of 'people caught in the toils of the truancy laws,' none of which is concerned with children's freedom (or the lack of it). Five refer to the problem of parents who wish their children to be taught to share their own religious beliefs, and three are about inferior schools. Children are mentioned only as people that 'you' (the parent) want to do something to while 'they' (the state) try to stop you. Whether the something that 'you' want to do is right or not is not questioned. It is assumed that if you are a parent then it is your right to decide, and that this is one of the most valuable freedoms that exists, more valuable than freedom for children or than the freedom for all concerned members of a democratic society to take part in the decisions about the sort of education that should be provided for the young. What is being argued in Rickenbacker's book is for greater freedom for parents to make decisions about what their children shall do, and less freedom for the state, but it is argued simply in the name of freedom. Rickenbacker claims to be against compulsion, saying:

> To many who support compulsory schooling, the use of compulsion is necessary to bring up the young to respect and practise the virtues and customs of society. To the critics of compulsory schooling it is precisely this coercive intrusion into the life and mind of the individual that represents the most damnable feature of compulsory schooling.[20]

However, like Rothbard, he ignores the fact that it is not only schools that 'intrude' into the lives and minds of children, and that children of parents who belong to the diverse groups he mentions are also brought up to respect and practise the virtues and customs of their particular group. If this is coercive then it is suffered by all children in every society, and if it is wrong then Rickenbacker should be as worried about parental intrusion as he is about compulsory schooling.

Diversity and Freedom

There is, in several of the essays in Rickenbacker's book, a confusion between freedom and cultural diversity. For example, the introduction to one essay says of its writer 'He discovers a heartening — but shaky — trend towards diversity, freedom and sovereignty of parents,'[21] which suggests, quite wrongly, that children's freedom and the sovereignty of parents go together, along with diversity. The *possibility* of diversity is necessary for freedom but its existence is not sufficient to guarantee freedom. If all the diverse groups in a society were to keep to themselves, mix with no-one else, and educate their children to do just the same there would be diversity of life-styles but less freedom. For freedom to exist it is necessary that people are able to *choose* between some of the many different beliefs and ways of living that exist. It is a matter of argument as to how many alternatives should be available for freedom to exist. John White suggests that children should learn about as many different activities as possible.[22] I would argue that it may be better for children to gain a deeper acquaintance with a few activities than to have a superficial knowledge of many. But whichever view is taken, some choice must exist if there is to be any freedom.

The fact that a boy who is brought up in St. Helens will be immersed in Rugby League, a Liverpudlian in football, a Barbadian in cricket and an American in baseball, basketball or American football, rather than all of them being able to choose from all of the sports, does not seem to me to be an important restriction of their liberty. We grow up within a community, with its own customs, and it is not necessary for our freedom for us to have every possible activity enjoyed by other communities laid before us as if on a super-market shelf. It would be a restriction of liberty, however, and an important one, if we were prevented from learning about or practising some possible alternative activities or ways of life. A girl from any of the above communities, for example, who was not allowed to play any of the games mentioned, or any others because the available funds had been used for boys' games, would have her freedom restricted. So would children who were prevented from learning about the games, or, more importantly, the beliefs and ways of life of other communities within their society. The diversity in a country which has Protestants and Catholics, atheists and Anglicans will not result in an increase of freedom for children unless they have some knowledge of the other groups and a chance to join them.

For many children, schools show the possibilities of different ways of life that their parents are unable or unwilling to reveal. However, for those who oppose compulsory education in the name of the sovereignty of the parent it is the chance that children will be exposed to other ideas and come to disagree with their parents, that they dislike and wish to avoid. The critics who take this view are really critics of state education rather than compulsory education, for they support the existence of private and religious schools and hold them up as an example of freedom. If we consider what goes on inside these schools, however, rather than concentrate on the fact of their existence, it is far from obvious that they increase freedom.

There is one contributor to this collection of essays who says 'it might be a good idea to ask kids what they think' but this suggestion is not pursued. Instead the author, Robert Baker, returns to the subject of the freedom of their parents, saying, of the Amish community (who wanted their children to leave school at the age of 14):

> What the Amish fear most is that their children, particularly teen-agers, will be lured away from their culture by the temptations abounding in the modern consolidated school.[24]

It is understandable that they have this fear. I had similar fears myself when I saw my own children exposed to pervasive and persuasive views that I believed to be wrong and dangerous. This is understandable parental concern and, as I have argued, there is a case to be made for adults protecting children from danger. What cannot be done, I maintain, is for this case to be made in the name of liberty. Underlying the concern about the restriction of parents' liberty is not a simple love of liberty but the belief that parents' freedom is more valuable than any benefits to their own children, to other children or to society as a whole that might accrue from universal compulsory education, including the possible benefit of increased and enhanced freedom for their children in the future.

The Failure of Compulsory Education to Deliver the Goods

A more impressive line of criticism of compulsory education comes from those who are concerned that schools frequently fail to achieve their aim of educating children. Such critics may concede that what the educators wish to achieve is valuable, but they believe it has not been achieved and, indeed, cannot be achieved by compulsion. As Goodman, one of the foremost critics of compulsory education, says 'since schooling undertakes to be compulsory must it not continually review its claim to be useful,'[25] and certainly if children's freedom is restricted on the grounds that they need to be taught particular skills and knowledge, then for paternalistic intervention to be justified it is necessary that they do learn them. Making children spend a large part of their time in the classroom is not a self-evidently acceptable practice, and if it is to be justified on the grounds that it achieves certain results we should be ever-watchful to ensure that it does achieve them (or achieves them better than possible alternative methods). The parenthesis is reasonable, for it is not necessary to show that schools are perfect and that all children know all they need to know for the present system to be justified. What is required is that the system achieves or could achieve its ends better than the alternatives now on offer or possible in the foreseeable future. The claim that this is so is rejected by those who hold that compulsion and education are incompatible.

Is Compulsion Incompatible with Education?

The belief that compulsion gets in the way of good education is held both by 'deschoolers' and those who would prefer schools to remain but for attendance to be voluntary. Reimer, for example, wants to 'deschool' society completely so that individuals would be in charge of their own education, and would, thereby, become more powerful and less liable to exploitation.[26] He believes that everyone should find their own 'skill-models' from a directory and then make a contract to be taught what they wish to learn. The major criticism of this approach is that people obviously need to be skilful already to use such a system successfully. Using directories and making contracts are not innate abilities, and it is not unduly pessimistic to assume that the free market Reimer envisages would, like other free markets, be one which the more powerful and knowledgeable members of society would be able to use for their own benefit and in which the less experienced would be taken for a ride. Encyclopedia salesmen have already demonstrated that there is a lucrative trade to be done with parents who desire to help their children but are unsure how best to do so. Doubtless there would be many more enterprising salesmen eager to exploit concerned but unsure parents and their children in a society which saw education as a product to be advertised and sold, while the more clued-in and affluent parents were ensuring their children had an education which would enable them to maintain positions of power.[27]

In addition to the parents who may not know the best way to help their children, there are those who are unwilling to do so. These are in a minority but the consequences of leaving the education of their children entirely in their hands should be considered seriously, and one needs to ask what would happen to these children if they were left to find their own skill-models. Reimer says 'Perhaps the most important thing that individuals can do is to take back their responsibility for the education of their children'[28] but the education of children is not simply the responsibility of individuals, for children are neither private luxuries nor private burdens. Reimer does not say what should happen to the children of those parents who failed to do this; nor does he consider that the consequences of free individuals making contracts to teach and learn might be to put more and not less power into the hands of teachers.

At the moment teachers in state schools cannot choose their pupils any more than pupils can choose their teachers, and while Reimer considers the possible benefits of getting rid of bad teachers because no-one would want to employ them, he does not say what would happen to the less attractive pupils. According to the ideology of the free market I suppose they would be so keen to enrol with the best and most favoured teachers that they would work hard and never mess about in class again. What is much more likely to happen, I suggest, is that they would be passed around the less successful teachers. This can be seen to happen to a certain extent in the private education system, with the most popular private schools able to attract staff, choose their pupils and name their own terms while the less able or less amenable children have to go elsewhere. Reimer's concern for children whose freedom is restricted is one I share, but although the removal of some restrictions would necessarily increase some freedoms, I see no reason to suppose that these would be valuable and important freedoms, or that there would be an overall increase in people's freedom from exploitation and freedom to direct their own lives.

Snobbishness, Elitism and Concern for Other People's Children

The argument that if the education of children were left to themselves and their parents some children would suffer, and that it is better, therefore, to have compulsory education for all to protect those who might be at risk has been criticized as snobbish. It is always the other parents who would be unable or unwilling to organize their children's education, it is said — never the person arguing for compulsory education. However, this criticism might be levelled equally at those who support any law they have no urge to break. For example, as it is not the legal prohibition against mugging old ladies that holds me back from going on the rampage, it is snobbish of me to support such a law on the grounds that it helps protect those who need it and check those who might otherwise engage in this activity? If this is the case then, without snobbishness, we can support only those laws which proscribe the particular forms of anti-social behaviour which tempt us.

More importantly, however, the charge of snobbishness or élitism, whether fair or not, could be levelled only at those who would agree that the education of children is the responsibility of individual parents, but fear some might not carry it out. My claim is that the education and welfare of the younger members of a society are matters of concern for and the responsibility of the whole of that society, and not simply, as deschoolers and traditional upholders of the rights of parents seem to believe, of individual parents. This responsibility will not be carried out satisfactorily if we assume that justice for children lies in treating them either as competent, competing individualists in a society of other individualists who are all capable of fighting for their own interests, or as beings whose upbringing and education is the business of no-one but their parents.

Compulsory Education for Those Who Need It

What John Kleinig calls the 'protectionist' argument for compulsory schooling[29] — that education has to be compulsory in order to protect those children whose parents would otherwise neglect it — has also been criticized on the grounds that as not all children need protection (either from their parents' irresponsibility or from themselves and their own ignorance and inexperience) it is unfair to restrict the freedom of all and make them suffer for the defects of the few. Kleinig says:

> It is all very well to intervene in cases of manifest abuse and neglect. But such interventions do not need to take the form of compulsory schooling and certainly not compulsory schooling for all. Not all children need protection from their parents.[30]

Leonard Krimerman takes a similar view and considers the possibility of having schools that would operate much as our hospitals do today. 'People would be committed into them temporarily, under extraordinary circumstances, and for the most part voluntarily.[31] Kleinig appears to have physical neglect in mind, whereas Krimerman is considering some failure in rationality which needs treatment, but both advocate state intervention only in cases of proven need, because this is less of an intrusion into the individual's liberty than compulsion for all. There are, I believe, several weaknesses in their arguments.

Firstly, Krimerman's suggestion that schools could operate as hospitals do, treating people occasionally, voluntarily and for limited periods, does not take account of the very real differences between being ill and being in need of education. Being ill is abnormal, and not usually a matter of dispute because generally we know when we are ill and desire to do what is necessary to get better. Being ignorant, inexperienced or relatively irrational however, is, at a certain stage of our lives, the common human condition, although we may not be fully aware of it at the time, nor may we know best how to rectify the matter if we do recognise it. Krimerman seems to suggest that if parents do not educate their children satisfactorily and their deficiency becomes apparent, then the children would be subject to compulsory education until the wrong is put right. However, the administration of what he calls 'sporadic educational intervention' would create far greater unhappiness, I believe, than our present system of universal compulsion, and would make the traumas of the 11 Plus seem negligible and the process of taking children into care seem almost trouble free by comparison.

Neither the diagnosis nor the cure for irrationality is as simple as that for chicken pox, and it would be hard if not impossible for decisions about children and their parents to be free from cultural bias and value judgments. It would be impossible, also, to avoid the implication of moral condemnation of both parents and children when compulsory education was deemed to be necessary, and decisions which would have such a detrimental effect on the self-images of the people involved would undoubtedly be criticized and challenged in courts of appeal. It is hard to see whose freedom would be increased or who would benefit in any other way: the children whose parents chose to send them to school or keep them at home would have as little say in the matter as children usually do; those deemed to be in need of sporadic educational intervention would be subject to (or sentenced to) compulsory schooling; and presumably all children would be screened in some way to discover those in need of schooling. I believe the idea of a safety net to catch the children whose parents do not educate them would cause even more distress and be more unjust than a system which insists on education for all. However, this, like the belief that children would learn what they need to know in a non-compulsory or self-directed education system, cannot be verified or falsified without experiments on the people whose education and welfare is our concern.

Compulsory Education and Prevention of Harm

Gardner considers a slightly different, stricter protectionist argument which is to do with the protection of children, not from the consequences of having parents who cannot advise on, say, the best way of becoming a metallurgist, but on protection from physical harm.[32] This argument is based on the distinction between interfering with a person to prevent harm to themselves (which even Mill said was permissible in certain circumstances) and interfering to promote their good.[33] Prevention of harm could be said to require that children learn to read, Gardner claims, but 'it is not an argument for the analysis of poetry or writing free verse or for studying Shakespeare.'[34] John White also uses the argument that prevention from harm justifies compulsion,[35] but he interprets 'harm' rather loosely, saying:

If children were left free not to have to speak, study mathematics, physics, philosophy or contemplate works of art, then this might well harm them, since they might never come to know whole areas of possible wants.[36]

For White, to be ignorant of any of the category one activities that one might wish to choose to pursue is to be harmed, but this is as mistaken, I suggest, as saying that we are harmed if we are deprived of any of the many foods we might choose. White does not claim that physics, mathematics, art appreciation etc. are all essential to a fully autonomous life. If he could show this, then his claim that ignorance of them constitutes harm might be upheld, but as it is he is quite happy for children to learn maths and philosophy, say, and then drop them completely having realized that they do not wish to engage in those activities, because the Good for them is music and poetry, or rugby and cricket. It is surely stretching the meaning of 'harm' to unacceptable lengths to count ignorance of something that a person might have wanted to do, but did not, as necessarily harmful for them.

White also refers to the possible harm to others if children are left ignorant of category one activities, for he considers that people who do not know of possible options and different ways of life may not be tolerant of those who choose differently from themselves. Therefore, he claims, it is in everyone's interest that all are taught to understand the category one activities and the different possible ways of life. I am unconvinced that someone who had learned something about an activity or way of life and then rejected it would necessarily be more tolerant of those who continued to pursue it than someone who knew nothing of it at all. However, my main disagreement with White's argument is that, having used a very wide interpretation of 'harm' with regard to category one activities, he excludes category two activities completely. If we are to justify compulsion in education on the grounds of preventing harm, then many category two activities must surely be included. More obvious harm is done both to the individual concerned and to others through ignorance of nutrition, child-care, first-aid, the highway code, or car maintenance etc. than through ignorance of art appreciation. If 'the principle of liberty may be overridden . . . to prevent harm both to the pupils themselves and to men in general'[37] then many of the practical subjects that make up White's category two activities will have to be included in a compulsory curriculum.

I have claimed that our responsibilities towards each other go beyond the mere prevention of harm, but even if this were not so, and even if it were easy to draw the line between preventing harm and promoting good, I do not believe schools could restrict themselves to teaching what is needed to prevent harm. We cannot teach children to reason, think critically or even read without getting them to reason, think critically or read about something, and that 'something' which is the subject matter will teach lessons of its own. We cannot separate the necessary skill from the 'something': we cannot legitimately extend children's language for an hour and then illegitimately get them to do leaf prints. It is while they pick the leaves, put on their aprons, mix their colours and set to work that their use of language can be extended. It would be possible, perhaps, to have an English syllabus which started with reading the instructions on fireworks and the Government Health Warnings on cigarettes, went on to the list of additives in orange squash and finished with the submissions to a public enquiry on the building of a nuclear reactor. Such a syllabus, however useful, would neglect vast areas of human experience which, though not necessary to physical survival, children do need to understand if they are to be able to participate fully in their society. In addition, a curriculum based on harm-prevention would contain some of what is in children's interest to know, but it would be no more (and probably even less) likely to interest them than their present curriculum.

Compensation for Coercion

It could be questioned whether it matters if children are bored if they are being protected from harm, but if they are being bored unnecessarily, and if, being bored they 'switch off' and are less likely to learn, and if boring schools are perceived as more oppressive than interesting ones, then it does matter. If we regretfully decide it is necessary to restrict children's freedom by compelling attendance at school, then we should compensate for that as far as we can by making their time there as interesting and pleasant as possible while still achieving the purpose. We cannot do either of these if we concentrate solely on contraception and the Green Cross Code, important though they are, and outlaw major parts of our culture such as music and fiction.

However, even if school is pleasant and interesting, if it is compulsory it will restrict children's freedom. The suggestion that if children can choose what they do in school their liberty is not restricted[38] is rightly criticized by Gardner on the grounds that want–satisfaction is not the same as freedom, for if it were we could be free simply by not wanting what we could not have.[39] Gardner says:

> Even if . . . pupils have their so-called free days, and their elective
> curriculum and want the options offered, some options, such as that
> of opting out of the whole enterprise and the range of alternatives for
> which this is necessary, are not available, hence the system interferes
> with freedom.[40]

This is so, but what Gardner appears to overlook is that we are never either
completely free or totally enslaved, but may be more or less free. Having to go
to school is one infringement of liberty, but, once there, having to study
Maths, wear a tie and not talk in the dinner queue are additional restrictions.
Being allowed to choose between activities and pursue one's own interests
within a compulsory system is not complete freedom, any more than being
educated by one's parents would be, but each is an example of limited freedom.

The subject of children's freedom within school will be considered in
more detail in the next chapter. I wish now only to make the point that a compulsory system inevitably restricts children's freedom, though not necessarily
more than the available alternatives, but that it need not be oppressive and that
restrictions should be kept to as few as possible. Unless it can be shown that
the practices listed by Robert Baker such as drugging children,[41] insisting they
are immunised,[42] requiring attendance at religious or flag-saluting cere-
monies,[43] beating them or simply teaching them badly are necessarily connected with compulsory education, then these are separate (though important)
issues which do not effect the principle of whether a society is justified in
ensuring that all its young members are educated. The practices of individual
schools or education systems in any particular society should not be taken as a
criticism of compulsory education as such, any more than a defence of compulsion should be mistaken for satisfaction with our present system.

Conclusion

Much of the criticism of compulsory schooling is basically criticism of what is
done in schools rather than of the principle of compulsion, but it is argued
sometimes that compulsion and education are necessarily incompatible.
Though it is possible to compel children to attend school, it is claimed, it is not
possible to compel them to learn, for learning is something that we have to do
for ourselves when we want to. It is true that no-one else can do our learning
for us. Learning is never a passive process, for when we know and understand

something — even if it is something we have been told or have read — we fit it into our existing framework of knowledge and actively make it our own. It is also true that when we are motivated and interested we learn more avidly. However, what follows from that is not that learning and compulsory school attendance are incompatible but that if we want children to learn more easily we have to motivate and interest them. Whether or not children are able to learn in a compulsory education system is a fact, and from the empirical evidence that there are many original and creative people who are products of such a system I conclude that compulsion and education are not incompatible. According to deschoolers and some other critics of compulsory education, children who are not made to go to school will learn what interests them and it seems to be assumed that what interests them is what they need to know. I question the belief that interest and need will coincide so conveniently. Reimer lists many things that people ought to know about the way society is organized and power distributed,[44] but though I would agree with him that these are important, I would argue that he is over-optimistic if he believes either that all children will want to learn them, or that this information will come their way in the free market he advocates.

Those who believe that children need only to be left alone in order to develop their talents are wrong on two counts. Firstly we have no reason to suppose that children left alone would blossom in this way. People are not like acorns which need only sun, water and space to grow into fine oaks: we need interaction with interested and interesting people.[45] Secondly children are not and will not be left alone. They will learn something from someone, and it is the duty of adults to ensure they learn what is worthwhile and what they will need to know rather than what they chance upon or what it is someone else's interest they should learn. To argue that children should be left free to decide what they want and need to know is to exhibit the naive liberal view of free choice which ignores the extent to which choices may be shaped, influenced or deliberately manipulated. If those who want children to understand their society and to be able to make choices both as individuals and as participants in a free society stand aside, then those who want to exploit or manipulate them will find the field free.

I have argued that the liberal view of human beings as individuals who come together only when it is in their interest to do so and have only the obligations they have chosen is a mistaken one. We are social beings whose responsibilities and obligations to our fellows, including caring for the young, exist whether we want them or not, and while parents undoubtedly do have responsibility for their children, they are not the only people who have. Children do not just belong to their parents and family, they are also young members of a wider community which has both an interest in and responsibility for the way they are educated. This is not a backdoor way of saying that children belong to the state instead of their parents. They do not 'belong' to anyone in the sense of being possessions, but they, like the rest of us, are social beings as well as individuals, and members of a wider community as well as members of a family. Thus while the community has a responsibility to promote and protect children's best interests, the children, as members of the community, are not just recipients of welfare but people with their own part to play, and contribution to make. Being educated is a child's current contribution to society as well as being preparation for future participation.

I can find no good reason to say that the legitimate role of the state should be limited to repelling external threats and enforcing contracts, and not extended to promoting good in other ways. It is reasonable to suggest that the state should be involved in the education of its younger members, both for their benefit and for the benefit of the wider community, and that it should not be left to chance or to individual parents to see that they learn what they need to know. All societies have some arrangement for the care and education of their young members and in all societies children are expected to learn and are not given the opportunity to opt out. Children must learn, just as adults must teach and care for them, and these are responsibilities that neither can shirk. What they learn should, in a free, democratic society be of concern to all, and a matter of public debate, as decisions about the sort of education we give our children affect the sort of society we have. If we value freedom we will want to ensure that all children are taught the necessary skills, attitudes and knowledge so that they too can make free choices, take part in the public decisions that affect all, and minimize the power that others are able to exercise over them. How their learning is organized should also be discussed. It might be that a non-compulsory education system could cater successfully for all children in a society in which power was more equally distributed than our own, and in which the freedom of parents to mould their children in their own image by denying them access to alternatives was not valued. Until that is achieved I would argue that, with all the acknowledged faults of our present system, compulsory education goes some way towards minimizing the difference in life chances between children whose parents are themselves educated and those who are not. Abolishing schools, or having them only for those children whose parents wanted them would not improve matters for the most disadvantaged children, nor would it make them, or any other children, more free. The major gain in freedom would be for the parents who wished to be in sole control of decisions made on behalf of their own children. This is not a freedom that I think should be valued highly.

Notes and References

1. It should be noted that much of what has been written about compulsory education comes from the United States, and that their school attendance laws differ from ours and vary from state to state. I have not dwelt on these differences between two countries which both claim to be freedom-loving democracies as they do not affect the principle of my argument.
2. M.S. Katz, 'Compulsion and the Discourse on Compulsory School Attendance' *Education Theory* 27
3. Ibid, p. 181
4. Ibid.
5. Peter Gardner, 'Liberty and Compulsory Eduation', in Phillips Griffiths *Of Liberty*
6. Ibid, p. 112
7. Ibid, p. 114
8. John Locke, *The Second Treatise of Government* p. 532
9. Gardner, op. cit. p. 122
10. Ibid.
11. Ibid.
12. Ibid, p. 110
13. Pat White, *Beyond Domination* p. 227
14. John White, *Towards a Compulsory Curriculum* p. 22
15. Ibid.
16. Ibid.
17. Murray N. Rothbard, 'Historical origins' in Rickenbacker, *The 12 Year Sentence*
18. John Holt, *Escape from Childhood* p. 185
19. Rickenbacker, op. cit.
20. Ibid, p. 2
21. Ibid, p. 59
22. John White, op. cit. p. 22
23. Robert P. Baker, 'Statute Law and Judicial Interpretations.' in Rickenbacker, op. cit. r. 130
24. Ibid, p. 120
25. Paul Goodman, *Compulsory Miseducation and the Community of Scholars*, p. 16
26. Everett Reimer, *School is Dead*

27. In their moving book *Letter to a Teacher* the boys of Barbiana show the injustice which results from an education system which is compulsory for only half the day, leaving the afternoons free for the better-off parents to arrange private tuition for their sons.
28. Reimer, op. cit. p. 158
29. John Kleinig, 'Compulsory Schooling.' *Journal of Philosophy of Education* 15
30. Ibid, p. 194
31. Leonard I. Krimerman, 'Compulsory Education: a Moral Critique.' in Strike and Egan, *Ethics and Educational Policy* p. 83
32. Gardner, op. cit.
33. Ibid, p. 125
34. Ibid, p. 126
35. John White, op. cit.
36. Ibid, p. 35
37. Ibid, p. 35
38. C. Bereiter, 'Moral Alternatives to Education.' *Interchange* 3 No. 1. p. 26 for example.
39 Gardner, op. cit.
40. Ibid, p. 30
41. See Holt, op. cit. p. 65
42. See Baker, op. cit. p. 117ff
43. Ibid, p. 110ff
44. Reimer, op. cit.
45. I am *not* suggesting that all teachers or only teachers are interested or interesting.

Chapter 9

Freedom in Schools

I have claimed that although restrictions of children's freedom are sometimes justified, this is not because children are inherently subject to adults' authority, or incapable of freedom or in some way less worthy of respect and consideration than adults. Restrictions of children's liberty are just as important as restrictions of adults' liberty and must be justified on broadly the same grounds and according to the same general criteria. I argued in the previous chapter that citizens of a democracy need to be educated in order to survive in, take part in, contribute to and benefit from their society, and that a democracy needs educated citizens in order to continue to operate as a democracy. I concluded that a system of compulsory education was justified in principle, although the legitimacy of compulsory education does not entail either the right of adults to impose their own wishes on children, or justify the unlimited restriction of children's freedom.

However the problems of children's freedom and their education are not simply those of compulsory attendance. We also must decide to what extent we may restrict the freedom of children within the schools which we compel them to attend. (As my son once put it 'I think it's right that we have to go, but it doesn't have to be such a dictatorship when we get there.')[1] The two are not completely separate problems, for there is certainly a connection between what is done with children in school and the question of whether compulsory education is justified. If compulsion is justified on the grounds that it achieves certain results, then it must work towards the achievement of those results, and will not be justified if it does not go some way towards their achievement. It would not be right to keep children in schools, for example, on the grounds that their freedom may justifiably be restricted in order that they may be taught what they need to know to take their places as members of a free, democratic society, if really they were being trained to be merely tractable consumers and obedient wage-slaves. If present restriction is justified on the grounds that it will enhance future freedom, then the education provided must have this as one of its aims, and must work towards its realization, for compulsion is never a good in itself. It may be justified to achieve certain important ends, while other ends would not count as sufficiently worthwhile or important to justify a restriction of freedom.

Having argued in the previous chapter that compulsory education is justifiable, I now wish to look more closely at the question of liberty within a compulsory education system, and to consider how schools might respect children's present rights of liberty while continuing to educate their pupils and prepare them for future freedom also. The question of children's political liberty to participate in the organization of the school and the formulation of school rules will be considered in the final chapter on education and democracy. In this chapter I will consider two areas of freedom: academic freedom — the freedom of children to choose what to study (and what not to study), to direct their own learning, choose their own teachers and set their own academic standards; and personal freedom in areas such as those of dress, behaviour outside the classroom, and freedom of movement and expression within school.

Academic Freedom for Children

The usual argument for academic freedom is part of Mill's argument for other forms of freedom of expression and argument — that it is necessary for the advancement of human knowledge and the discovery of truth.[2] This would appear not to apply to children, for though they may discover much at school, the 'discovery learning' they do there is not, nor is intended to be, discovery of something which no-one else has ever thought of before. It is discovery of knowledge that is new to the child in a form that is more comprehensible and meaningful and therefore less easily forgotten. Until children have learned basic skills, standards of rationality and some factual knowledge they are most unlikely to advance human knowledge. If children are to have a form of academic freedom at school, then, it must be on grounds other than those used to justify it at a more advanced level — that they are human beings with their own lives to lead who have the right to pursue their own interests.

I have argued that our justification for compelling children to attend school (or receive an equivalent education elsewhere) is that there are certain things they need to know in order to survive in our society, to become part of the community and play their part in it, and to be able to make reasoned choices as individuals. If this is the case then clearly it would be inconsistent to allow children complete academic or personal freedom when they are at school if this meant they did not learn all that had been thought important enough to justify their compulsory attendance. Among those who have attempted to extend the liberty of children in school, either in progressive schools, free schools or the state system, there is a divergence of opinion about whether children should have complete academic freedom, and this difference appears to be based on different interpretations of the purpose of schools. Almost alone of libertarian teachers A.S. Neill maintained the position of allowing children complete freedom to choose whether they attend any lessons or none — a position which sprang from his views both on the purpose of education and on the nature of the child.

Neill believed that the purpose of a school was to enable children to be happy. Unlike many of the other pioneers of the new school or progressive education movement he did not want simply to find less oppressive ways of teaching, or more subtle ways of socializing and controlling children, and bringing them to share the values of their society or their teachers. He placed supreme importance on children being happy, and thought the way to make them so was to give them freedom. If they wanted to learn then they would do so, and if they did not then it was better for them to be happy as illiterate street sweepers. This view of the purpose of schools is inextricably linked to Neill's view of the nature of the child — neither of which I share. He said:

> We set out to make a school in which we should allow children freedom to be themselves. In order to do this we had to renounce all discipline, all direction, all suggestion, all moral training, all religious instruction . . . All that is required was what we had — a complete belief in the child as a good, not an evil being . . . My view is that a child is innately wise and realistic. If left to himself without adult suggestion of any kind he will develop as far as he is capable of developing.[3]

Briefly, on the subject of happiness, I would argue that although it is a good it is not the only good, and even if it were, a school that made happiness its sole aim would still face a conflict between catering for children's present happiness or that of the future. The happiness of doing no lessons and learning nothing that is not of immediate appeal may preclude later satisfactions, and the freedom to stay away from lessons will then seem to have been less valuable. We are brought back again and again to the problem of the relative value of different freedoms, and the conflict between Locke's 'unrestrain'd liberty'[4] or what Simone Weil calls 'an unconditional surrender to caprice'[5], and the freedom of being able to make one's plans and being capable of carrying them through. In her theoretical picture of a free society[6] Weil contrasts the freedom which little children would enjoy if parents did not impose any rules on them with the freedom of being able to order one's own actions. The former is to do with desire and its satisfaction, whereas the latter is concerned with thought and purpose which can be translated into action. While accepting that the free society and the free man are unrealizable ideals, she says:

> the absolutely free man would be he whose every action proceeded from a preliminary judgment concerning the end which he set himself, and the sequence of means suitable for attaining this end.[7]

It would be hard for a child to conceive of that kind of freedom, without having had some stimulating interaction with adults, or to be able to use it without having certain skills that are not always learned incidentally.

As was argued in the previous chapter, children are not, as Neill believed, like plants which grow to their own particular pre-determined pattern unless their growth is stunted in some way. They may manage without adult dictation, and perhaps without adult direction, but Neill's assertion that they will develop their full potential without adult suggestion of any kind is false. For example, children who are trained as gymnasts, tennis players or violinists reach levels of competence that far exceed those of the untrained enthusiasts. Whether it is *right* to train children to such high levels in this way is debatable, but there can be no doubt that training for certain skills leads to greater achievement; that what one achieves must be within one's potential; and that, therefore, leaving children without adult suggestion of any kind will not enable them to go as far as they are able.

Again, as was argued in the previous chapter, however hard schools and teachers might try not to suggest anything to their pupils, children are surrounded by other influences. Even Summerhill children went to the cinema each week, home for the holidays, and probably read books and comics, and these outside influences would affect the inclinations that Neill considered to be innate. Neill admitted that the freedom of Summerhill worked best for the intelligent children,[8] for when they decided to work for external exams they were able to tackle the intensive work required in a short time. It seems highly probable that these children had been exposed also to some adult suggestion — or at least some adult enthusiasm — perhaps from their parents, and that this had stimulated their intelligence as well as motivating them to want to pass their exams. For Neill, children without academic interests and girls who did not attend Maths or Physics lessons were simply expressing their own natures, and not only should not be forced to go but should not be encouraged either as:

> It is an absurd curriculum that makes a prospective dressmaker study quadratic equations or Boyle's law.[9]

This is a deterministic view of children's potential and their future lives, and it does nothing to counteract the influence and expectations of the particular section of society in which the children grow up.

If the interests which children are free to pursue (which affect the choices they will be able to make as adults) are left entirely to them, they will be based on limited knowledge and experience and influenced by all the voices of persuasion except those of their teachers. As Dewey put it:

> The suggestion upon which pupils act must . . . come from somewhere. It is impossible to understand that a suggestion from one who has a larger experience and a wider horizon should not be at least as valid as a suggestion arising from some more or less accidental source.[10]

I have often noticed that when young children without wide experience are given a completely free choice of activity at school they copy the first child who has an idea of what to do. However, if several suggestions for possible activities are sought by the teacher and considered by the children before the choice has to be made, then the children do not all end up doing the same thing. In such circumstances adult suggestion, or adult instigation, which might theoretically be thought to narrow the range of choice and limit freedom, in fact enlarges it. It is important to help children to determine for themselves what they would like to do, what they need to know next and how to go about pursuing their individual investigations, but until they are equipped with the necessary skills and knowledge for this they should not be allowed complete academic freedom. The freedom to choose what line of study to pursue and how best to pursue it is inappropriate for children whose intellectual skills are relatively underdeveloped and who have insufficient experience to know what choices are available.

In contrast to the philosophy of Neill and Summerhill, most private Free Schools, progressive schools and free(ish) schools within the state system, do not allow pupils complete freedom to choose what, if anything, they wish to study. In his sympathetically critical study of private free schools, Allen Graubard reports that the longer such schools are in existence the more likely they are to have some sort of arrangement for attendance at lessons.[11] Some have contracts arranged between the pupils and teachers for a course of lessons. Some insist on attendance at a core of important lessons. In a British state school, Countesthorpe College, a system was tried in which the pupils were responsible for determining the choice and direction of their own courses of study but they had to do this together with the teachers, and in consequence gained valuable experience of planning their own work. Two of the teachers say:

> The task we set ourselves was to create the conditions in which autonomy could thrive. We did not intend meekly to submit to each student's passing whims and fancies, for unless teachers are ready to be positive, forceful and ambitious in their expectations of their students they cannot hope to create the conditions for a thriving autonomy.[12]

It is neither coercive nor oppressive to point out to children that courses do not write themselves. If teachers prepare work on a subject that the children have chosen, then the children should turn up and do their part as well.

Teachers working with pupils who come from homes or communities where there is little expectation of academic success should provide the counter-suggestion that academic success is a possibility and that careers may be open to students other than those which seem most obvious. I am not suggesting that teachers should hold up middle class culture and jobs as the most worthwhile or desirable, or attempt to recruit the most able working class pupils into the middle class. However, if children are to choose what they will do as adults, they must be aware of the possibilities, and that may include possibilities that had not previously occurred to the children or their parents. They will also need to know what standards will be required of them, and whether they are on the way to reaching them. It is dispiriting for people, after months or years of thinking that they are doing fine, to find that in fact they are not. For children from affluent homes who attend private free or progressive schools, the teachers' role in extending the children's academic abilities and preparing them for a variety of different careers may not be particularly important. Such schools are sometimes somewhat disdainful of examination results. Perhaps they can afford this attitude because their ex-pupils will not find it difficult to retake the places in society that they have left. State schools and those American private free schools which cater for working class and black children, on the other hand, cannot be little islands of rural peace which take no account of the realities and politics of modern urban society.

The case that more rigorous teaching in hard subjects is needed in such schools is put with particular force by Jonathon Kozol, because of his experience with black free schools in the United States. He says:

> It is too often the rich white kids who speak three languages with native fluency at the price of sixteen years of high-cost, rigorous and sequential education, who are the most determined that poor kids should make clay vases, weave Indian headbands, play with Polaroid cameras, climb over geodesic domes[13]

and he also draws attention to the fact that education is not simply a matter of benefiting individuals and helping them to make a success of their lives, but of providing the rest of the community with the skilled practitioners it needs.

> Harlem does not need a new generation of radical basket-weavers. It does need radical, strong, subversive, steadfast, skeptical, rage-minded and powerwielding obstetricians, pediatricians, lab technicians, defense attorneys, Building Code examiners, brain surgeons.[14]

Kozol's point reminds us that education for free individuals and a free society is not simply a matter of individuals hearing about the possible opportunities that exist, and learning the skills necessary to avail themselves of them. In order to be free we must not be subject to the power of those who would exploit us, and keeping this freedom is a political matter.

Teachers who are concerned about extending the liberty of children, then, do not have to avoid suggestions or even direct instruction. They should not fall into the common mistakes made by many teachers in free schools of assuming firstly that because some learning is incidental, all learning is incidental, and secondly that any learning is as good as any other.[15] There may, indeed there will, be occasions when it will be necessary to insist that children study subjects they would rather not, for, as has been said, if some knowledge is important enough for us to insist that children attend school to learn it, it would be inconsistent to allow them to choose not to learn it. However, this does not mean that children should have no academic freedom at all, for they, like most other people, learn better when they want to and when they are interested. If children are allowed to find out things for themselves and pursue their own enquiries, although it is unlikely to bring an increase in knowledge and understanding to the whole society, it will bring it to the individual, and it will also give valuable structured experience of independent study and individual choice. As children get older they will be able to discuss with their teachers what they need and would like to learn, as the pupils did at Countesthorpe College.

It must be reiterated that though compulsion and restriction may be justified to achieve certain ends, there can be no justification for unnecessary or excessive restrictions. Therefore, whenever there is the possibility of both achieving the end and allowing freedom this should be done. If, for example, it is considered important that children learn to write, then even if they could learn just as readily by writing what did not interest them as what did, there would be no justification for restricting their writing to the teacher's interests rather than their own. In fact, as most teachers know, it is far more effective to use, encourage and build on children's own interests as a way of helping them to learn, and so while teachers keep clear in their own minds what needs to be learned the child is allowed as much freedom of choice as possible within the necessary constraints. Advocates of free schooling might criticize this for giving children an illusion of freedom rather than the real thing, for the children are given to understand they are choosing for themselves whereas in reality they are just following the teacher's pre-ordained plan. However, if part of the teacher's and our society's plan is that children should sometimes be free to follow their own interests, the freedom would not be all illusory. Nor would it simply be a case of the teacher choosing the ends while the children were allowed to choose some of the means.

Education is much too complex a process for us to describe it simply in terms of means and ends and say, for example, the end is that children learn to write, and that their stories and projects are no more than the means to that end, or that the work they choose for themselves and do on their own is no more than the means to the end of learning to work independently. The importance of the child's present as well as of preparation for the future was stressed by Dewey, who said:

> When preparation is made the controlling end, then the potentialities of the present are sacrificed to a suppositious future. When this happens the actual preparation for the future is missed or distorted. The ideal of using the present simply to get ready for the future contradicts itself . . . We only live at the time we live and not at some other time, and only by extracting at each present time the full meaning of each present experience are we prepared for doing the same thing in the future. This is the only preparation which in the long run amounts to anything.[16]

When young children choose to work on a topic that interests them, or when older pupils select the school subjects they want or need to study, they are not simply choosing the means to an end chosen by someone else: they are both exercising freedom at that time and preparing for other exercises of freedom in the future.

On the subject of children's academic freedom I would conclude firstly, that children should not be given complete academic freedom, but should have as much as possible without neglecting what we have deemed they should know; secondly, that this has the practical advantage of promoting their learning; thirdly, that even if this were not the case, unnecessary restrictions on their freedom would not be justified; and finally that amongst the important things they need to learn are how to find out information for themselves, study independently, pursue interests and undertake work for purposes other than that of pleasing their teacher. They cannot do this, or develop into people who can use a fuller form of academic freedom, without having the opportunity to practise: nor can they develop fully, intellectually or socially, without the stimulation of interaction with concerned adults. However anxious teachers and parents are for their children to be free, they must not simply stand aside, fearing that their influence would be restrictive, for, as Dewey said:

> All human experience is ultimately social . . . it involves contact and communication. The mature person, to put it in moral terms, has no

right to withhold from the young on given occasions whatever capacity for sympathetic understanding his own experience has given him.[17]

Social and Personal Freedom in School

Schools are social institutions as well as educational ones, and many of the rules and restrictions of children's freedom at school are not directly concerned with their studies at all, but with their behaviour. If certain restrictions on children's freedom to choose what they will and will not study are justified in order that they should learn important skills, principles and facts, then on the grounds that willing the end involves willing the means, restrictions on behaviour which are necessary in order that this learning can take place will also be justified. There will, of course, be disagreement about which restrictions are necessary to maintain, in a community of young people, the conditions necessary for learning. When I was at school my teachers appeared to think that the necessary order would be destroyed if we ate sweets in school uniform or removed our hats on the bus. It was then considered reasonable (though not by the pupils!) for teachers to restrict behaviour outside school. More recently, my own children who had been educated perfectly adequately in jeans and jerseys all through primary school were suddenly, at the age of eleven, thought to need the help of a navy blue skirt or a blazer and tie if they were to continue learning. There are many such restrictions of children's freedom in our schools which are neither necessary to promote or facilitate learning, either directly or by promoting the good order and cooperative behaviour necessary in a community, nor necessary to keep children safe. Such restrictions, I claim, are not justified.

It is on the subject of discipline and children's behaviour that schools which attempt to extend children's freedom are most frequently criticized. Having read of the criticism by parents, press and governors of state schools such as William Tyndale Junior School,[18] Risinghill Comprehensive,[19] Countesthorpe College[20] and others, it is hard to escape the cynical conclusion that many of the critics would not have minded if the children had learned nothing, as long as they had done it quietly and unobtrusively. Some of the problems of children's behaviour that free private and state schools have appear to arise from the fact that they have a disproportionate number of particularly difficult or disturbed children. Some parents sent their children to Summerhill specifically for help with their psychological problems, and then removed them to more structured schools when they had improved. Both Risinghill and William Tyndale made efforts to retain and help difficult pupils instead of merely containing them or moving them elsewhere. This concern for difficult children is admirable, but it seems probable that because of the numbers of problem children in free schools teachers there are liable sometimes to confuse the freedom that should be given to normal children with the particular licence that a disturbed pupil may need in certain circumstances.

Neill himself clearly differentiated between the roles of doctor and fellow citizen, (as I would do between doctor or social worker and teacher), saying that the self-regulation he wanted children to achieve did not mean being free to destroy and upset others, and that:

> The whole freedom movement is marred and despised because so many advocates of freedom have not got their feet on the ground...It is true that I have spent a good few years of my life patiently tolerating the destructive behaviour of problem children, but I did this as their psychological doctor and not as their fellow citizen.[21]

The rights and liberty that children should have in a school that values freedom should, like the rights and liberties we would enjoy in a free society, never include the freedom to destroy property,[22] disrupt others' opportunities to learn, or to terrorize the neighbourhood. The problem for teachers, as for all those who are involved in organizing democratic societies or institutions, is how to respect individual rights to liberty and yet prevent infringements of the rights of others. In order to do this they will need to consider what the school rules should be, and how to make them the kind of rules which, it was argued in Chapter 4, can enlarge total liberty rather than diminish it.

First thoughts would suggest that the children in a school with few rules would be freer than those in a school with many rules, but of course it is the scope of the rules rather than their number which affects how restrictive they are. The rule that 'children must behave sensibly at all times' is far more pervasive, and more difficult to keep, than a number of explicit rules stating where and when bicycles may be ridden, or chocolate eaten. Again, the rule that forbids is less restrictive than the one which commands, for if you are, for example, forbidden to wear stiletto heeled shoes, then presumably you may wear any other type of shoe; whereas if the rule enjoins the wearing of a brown flat sandal with a T bar strap, then very little room is left for individual choice. Because of this, it has been argued that school rules should forbid rather than command[23] and should be explicit rather than all-embracing.[24] However, while appreciating the need for children to have clear guidelines for certain circumstances, I would argue that to rely on this form of rule on the grounds that it is less restrictive would be to give too much importance to the quantity of freedom that children could enjoy, and not enough to the quality.

Schools may feel the need of some 'Highway Code' type of rules to avoid large numbers of children charging into each other in the corridors, but what they really want to establish is a community in which the children are aware of the needs of others, and therefore move around in a way that does not disturb other people. The rule that forbids running in the corridor is explicit, easily understood and less restrictive than an expectation of careful and considerate movement at all times. However, unfortunately, such narrow, clear rules do not help the children towards self-discipline, and they may encourage attention to the letter of the law rather than its spirit. Holt is right to stress the evil of seemingly arbitrary or retrospective laws which leave children anxious and unsure of whether they may inadvertently commit a crime.[25] However, the aim of promoting self-discipline and protecting the rights of others, will not be achieved by having narrow, explicit rules that forbid. It will be necessary to show how these rules fit into broad principles of behaviour, and it is the quality of the relationships between teachers and pupils, rather than school rules, which will play the major part in regulating behaviour in a free and cooperative educational community.

A recurring theme in the comments made by children who have attended free schools, state or private, is their appreciation of being respected by their teachers as equals in importance, if not in knowledge and experience — a respect which they believe is not shown in more authoritarian schools.[26] Perhaps, as adults, if we are fortunate enough to have become accustomed to respect, we may undervalue its importance to children, and will expect to find something more startling than equal respect as the basis for free schools and education for freedom. It may be necessary, then, to remember how many actions, not wrong in themselves, outrage some adults when done by children. Wearing short skirts, long skirts, bright shirts, black shirts, long hair, short hair and any sort of hat will upset some teachers, parents and governors, as will talking with hands in pockets, neglecting to say 'Sir' or expressing any opinion unasked. It would be salutary for any adult who thinks equal respect is not a tough enough concept to be fundamental to a free atmosphere in a school to spend a weeek in any modern, bright and not obviously repressive school, and discover how frequently it is lacking. In saying this I would not want to suggest that teachers are worse than everyone else. Often they show more respect for the young people they teach than others do. (We have all seen the person in the tobacconist's shop who expects to be served before the child buying sweets.)

Respect is shown, or not shown, of course, not only in what teachers say to pupils, and how they say it, but in the importance that is placed on what the pupils say themselves, and the spirit in which their contributions, in social or educational situations, are received. If children are respected as people with important ideas of their own, then what they say on the subject of restriction and freedom in school must be listened to, and the extent to which they should be free to share in the organizing and running of their school will be discussed in the next chapter.

Notes and References

1. David Chamberlin, at the age of twelve, about a school which was far from a dictatorship.
2. J.S. Mill, *On Liberty* p. 85
3. A.S. Neill, *Summerhill* p. 20
4. John Locke, *The Second Treatise of Government* p. 532
5. Simone Weil, *Oppression and Liberty* p. 85
6. Ibid, p. 83–108
7. Ibid, p. 85
8. Neill, op. cit. p. 112–113
9. Ibid, p. 39
10. John Dewey, *Education and Experience* p. 71
11. Allen Graubard, *Free the Children* p. 156-7
12. Michael Armstrong and Lesley King in Watts (ed) *The Countesthorpe Experience* p. 54
13. Jonathan Kozol, *Free Schools* p. 33
14. Ibid, p. 45
15. This point is made by Dewey, op. cit. p. 25
16. Ibid, p. 49
17. Ibid, p. 38
18. See John Gretton and Mark Jackson *William Tyndale: Collapse of a School – or a System?* and Terry Ellis and Brian Haddow, Dorothy McColgan and Jackie McWhirter *William Tyndale: the Teachers' Story*

19. Leila Berg, *Risinghill: Death of a Comprehensive*
20. Watts, op. cit.
21. Neill, op. cit. p. 105
22. Aware of children's potential for destructiveness Neill said 'Really any man or woman who tries to give children freedom should be a millionaire, for it is not fair that the natural carelessness of children should always be in conflict with the economic factor'. op. cit. p. 130
23. John Holt, *Freedom and Beyond* p. 25ff
24. Ibid, p. 27
25. Ibid.
26. See, for example, Graubard, op. cit. p. 70.

Chapter 10

Liberty, Democracy and Education

I have claimed that citizens of a democracy need to be educated in order to survive in, take part in, contribute to and benefit from their society, and that a democracy needs educated citizens in order to continue to operate as a democracy. As the universal education needed in a democracy would, most probably though not necessarily, be achieved through a compulsory education system, I concluded that compulsory education was justified, despite the fact that this restricts freedom. As democracy requires compulsory education, and compulsory education restricts freedom it was accepted that in this respect democracy restricts the liberty of children. However, that is only one aspect of the complex inter-relationship between liberty, education and democracy. In this, the final chapter, I will attempt to draw together my previous arguments about freedom and its relationship with democracy and relate them to the education of children in a democratic society, for a democratic society, and within a compulsory education system. First, it will be necessary to recapitulate earlier ideas on the relationship between liberty and democracy.

Democracy and Liberty

I argued in Chapter 3 that freedom and democracy are connected if for no other reasons than that a democracy allows people the opportunity to be involved in the making of political decisions if they so wish, and that, because of the opportunity it affords to remove any elected leaders who show dictatorial tendencies, it reduces the risk that they will be deprived of other important freedoms. It was claimed also that as discussion and the opportunity for dissent are essential elements of democracy, certain basic freedoms must be guaranteed to individuals and minorities as well as to the majority if democracy is to continue. Thus there is a positive relationship between democracy and liberty:

firstly because having the opportunity to take part in government is a freedom in itself; secondly, because there is a contingent relationship between freedom and democracy due to the fact that other valued freedoms are less likely to be taken from those who have some control over the making of political decisions and the distribution of power than from those who have not; and thirdly, because without the basic freedoms we require in order to participate in political life democracy could not continue. Thus, though democracy may require some restrictions of freedom it is also a form of freedom in itself, provides some safeguard for other freedoms, and could not survive without them.

Democracy and Education

The relationship between democracy and education is similarly complex, but can usefully be considered in three ways: education within a democratic society, education for a democratic society and democracy in schools. However, as will be seen, these three subjects overlap considerably. It will not be possible, or even desirable, to prevent discussion of one of these topics from flowing over into the others, for democracy in schools is part of education for democracy and both are essential elements of education within a democratic society. Schools and other educational institutions exist within a wider society, and because decisions about education, its distribution and content are political decisions, these will be made, in a democracy, with some degree of reference to or involvement by the citizens. I should emphasize at this point that when I say, for example, that 'we' consider certain knowledge important or decide that children should learn such-and-such, the 'we' refers to the whole community and not just to teachers, school governors or the DES. In a society more fully democratic than our own the content of the school curriculum would be a subject of discussion — a discussion in which, like those on other important subjects, children would be educated to participate when they were able. It is because schools are part of a wider society with a legitimate interest in its life that they cannot exist as little, isolated democratic states which pay no regard to the views or interests of the wider community.[1] However, at the same time as existing within a democratic society (which should treat education as a matter of interest and a crucial concern) schools are organizations with power structures of their own and their own internal decisions to be made. If they are to be democratic institutions then the people who work in them — staff and pupils — will be involved in the making of those decisions, and this participation will be educative as well as intrinsically worthwhile. Thus, members of a democratic society have an interest in and responsibility for education; education prepares children to play their part in the democratic society; an important part of education for democratic participation involves practical experience of democracy in school; and that practical experience of democracy is valuable in its own right, and not simply as a preparation for the future. Clearly, education in a democratic society, education for participation in a democratic society and democracy in schools are interconnected, but in as far as they can be separated I will begin with the first strand — education in a democratic society.

Education in a Democratic Society

As I stressed in Chapter 3, citizen participation and involvement — and not simply the election of leaders — are the essence of democracy. If this were not the case, and democracy was only the restricted, sterile exercise that Schumpeter favours,[2] then there would be little connection between it and education. With citizen involvement at a low level there would be no public discussion about the sort of schools and education required, or where in the list of priorities for government spending education should come. Prospective leaders might pick an education policy if they thought it would be popular and help in their search for votes, but this would only be part of their self-advertisement and not chosen to serve the interests of the children or of their society.

In a Schumpeterian democracy there would be little scope for democracy within the school either, for although theoretically there would be the possibility of the only democratic practices Schumpeter acknowledges — elections and open competition for positions of power — in practice it is unlikely that a society which places high value on leadership and efficiency and low value on the contribution of the mass of people would be one in which pupils elected their teachers, or teachers their Head. Decisions would be taken by the Head and senior staff then, who would have been appointed and not elected, and they would not have to devote much time to educating children to take part in a democratic society. The participation demanded in Schumpeter's democracy is so minimal that no-one would need to be educated for it. As all anyone, except the prospective leaders, would have to do is plump for one leader rather than another for no discernible reason except that they appeared to be a good leader, no knowledge would be necessary, no skill, no practice, and therefore no education for democracy.

A more fully democratic society, however, would place high value on educating the young, both as individuals with their own lives to lead and as participants in joint democratic decisions. High priority would need to be given to educational matters and there would have to be wide discussion of the curriculum and organization of schools. Greater participation and public involvement in a democratic society require education, and schools have an important part to play in preparing people for that involvement. Some may consider that educating people for democratic participation is Utopian, but people are more likely to be involved and active if they believe they have a realistic chance of influencing events, if the issue is important to them, and if they have been socialized or educated to participate. Members of the middle class are more likely to be involved in political movements than members of the working class, and unless it is believed that this is part of their genetic inheritance, we must assume that their enthusiasm for involvement has been learned. For a long time English public schools claimed to educate boys to be leaders, and, as so many of our leaders are products of those schools it may be assumed that their political education was successful in achieving its ends. Until we have tried as hard to educate all children to participate in our democratic institutions and cooperate in the running of our society we should not dismiss the majority of the population as incapable of participation.

Education for Democracy

Democratic participation at the micro level, in areas close to the individual, is always educational, but at work or in political or social organizations the education will be incidental, perhaps not even noticed by those whose object is to manufacture articles for sale, campaign for a community centre or organize a Mothers' and Toddlers' Club. In schools, however, where the purpose is to educate, the balance between participatory democracy in its own right, as a way of running an organization, and the educative aspect of participation would be different. Both aspects should still be present: participation in the school (or class) organization in order to learn how to take part in other and larger organizations, and participation for the same reasons that it is ever desirable — basically because it is right that people should join together to help make the decisions that will affect their lives, and to control the extent to which others have power over them. Nevertheless, we would expect that in school, more than in any other institution, the educative function would predominate, and not be incidental, and so special efforts would need to be made to teach children the knowledge, skills and attitudes that will enable them to play their part in the democratic organization of society.

The need for more and better political education has been argued convincingly and often — though to little effect. The Politics Association was founded in order to develop 'political literacy' in secondary school pupils, and in the mid-sixties the Newsom Report said:

> A man who is ignorant of the society in which he lives, who knows nothing of its place in the world and who has not thought about his place in it, is not a free man even though he has a vote. He is easy game for 'hidden persuaders'[3]

(amongst whom, I would argue, we would find Schumpeter's would-be leaders competing for power.) Yet even so, because of fears of bias and indoctrination, and perhaps because we do not value democratic participation highly enough, political education is all too often restricted to the learning of facts about the constitution and parliamentary procedure rather than being a preparation for participating in a democratic society. Our children's political education suffers from the fact that though, as a society, we claim to value democracy, we are extremely suspicious of politics! The right to vote may be valued, but the people who ask you to vote for them are not.

There are, I suggest, three strands to the sort of political education young people need in a democracy. Firstly, they will need a broad education which will teach them the skills and knowledge of our society and develop their intellect and understanding. Democracy cannot be practised in the abstract and all the experience in the world of debates, votes and elections will be useless without some understanding of the subjects being debated. Secondly, they will need more specific knowledge about political issues and institutions and the distribution of power in our society; and thirdly there will have to be practical education within the school of the workings of a democratic organization, for, as Mill said:

> We do not learn to read or write, to ride or swim, by being merely told how to do it, but by doing it, so it is only by practising popular government on a limited scale that the people will ever learn how to exercise it on a larger[4]

The purpose of organizing a school democratically, however, is not simply to prepare children for future involvement in democracies, though this is an important part. Children are not simply embryonic citizens, trainee democrats or even future individualists. They are people with current feelings and wants who feel oppressed or undervalued if their own views are silenced or ignored, or their own wants dismissed as unimportant or irrelevant, and so whenever possible they should be involved in the making of decisions that affect them, just as adults should. The relationship between education and democracy is not simply one of a preparation for future participation in a democratic society, with democratic participation in schools existing only for educative purposes. Democracy in schools is required in its own right. It is not easy to combine democratic activity for its own sake and education for democracy, but just as, for example, English or Music teachers try to provide opportunities for children to do work that is intrinsically worthwhile as well as being a good preparation for future work, so political education should provide opportunity for political activities that are valid in themselves as well as being educational.

I argued that children cannot be allowed the academic freedom to avoid learning the important things they need to know in order to survive in our society, to become part of the community and play their part in it, and to be able to make reasoned choices as individuals. Clearly then they cannot be allowed the political freedom to decide democratically that their school will become an institution with a different purpose. This is a restriction of their freedom, to which they might not consent if given the choice, but consent is not necessary to justify all obligations and restrictions of liberty, and if, in a free and democratic society, there are just restrictions of liberty, and non-contractual obligations to other members of society, then these may exist in a free and democratic school also. Children are no more free from the obligation to make some contribution to their society — a contribution which cannot be made from ignorance — than adults are. Despite that, there is much room for a great increase in participation by pupils in the running of their schools, and many more areas of common concern over which they can exercise democratic control. Increasing democracy in schools will not be a simple matter, as any attempts to do so will face all the problems common to any democratic institution, plus the particular problems associated with young people whose experience is relatively limited and whose rationality may not be fully developed. However, the discussion and resolution of common problems is an essential feature of democracy, and discussing and attempting to resolve problems in school is an essential part of education for and in a democratic society.

Democracy in School

One of the problems that all democratic organizations share is that of ensuring that those who take the decisions are responsible for the consequences, for it is clearly unfair if everyone votes to pursue one course of action and then responsibility for its failure is shouldered by one or two individuals. Seeing this problem as a barrier to the introduction of greater democracy in schools, Musgrove says:

> Responsibility is properly linked with power. Pupils are members of a school in a different sense and on different terms from their teachers. To be responsible is to be liable for punishment if things go wrong: pupils cannot be punished like their teachers for the failure of school policies even if they had a hand in shaping them. Their claim to a share in power is weak.[5]

However, Musgrove's conclusion results from his viewing the problem the wrong way round. Firstly we should recognize that pupils are deeply affected in important ways by decisions made in schools. Wrong decisions might damage a school's reputation or spoil a teacher's chance of promotion, but the most serious consequences fall on the pupils. If they are thought to be capable of participation, and of enjoying or suffering the results of that participation, their claim to a share of power is strong. So instead of saying that as pupils do not share responsibility they should not share power, we should approach from the other direction and say that as they are affected by decisions they should, if possible, share power, and that therefore we should try to devise ways to enable them to share responsibility also. The problem of correctly assigning responsibility for decisions and blame for mistakes is a real one, but it is a problem for all democratic organizations.

One way round the problem of sharing power and responsibility in our present education system is suggested by Peter Scrimshaw who says that greater democracy could be introduced in only those schools in which the head was willing to take the risk of allowing others to take decisions for which the head would still be legally responsible.[6] He imagines that democratic and conventional schools would co-exist and that people would choose the sort of organization they liked best — eventually being won over to the democratic schools. Unfortunately, with the decline in the number of school-age children and the cost, in time and money, of travel, I do not feel this is a practical suggestion in most areas of the country, for though the picture of people choosing between different schools has some attractions, the fact is that for most people there is no real choice. In a society which was less authoritarian and gave a higher priority to education for democracy than does our own, Scrimshaw's suggestion might be feasible, though in such a society it would hardly be necessary.

However Scrimshaw is right to say that heads who are willing to give up some power even though they will still be held legally responsible can introduce greater democratic participation in their schools. In some schools great efforts have been made to develop democracy, and much may be learned from their successes and failures. Perhaps, to start with there was too much emphasis on the outward forms of democracy such as electing representatives to a School Council with little real power. These often presented a façade of democracy which children came to mistrust. School Councils do have a useful part to play, but they seem to have been most successful in small private free schools where direct democracy could operate.

At Summerhill, for example, Neill, all teachers, and the pupils over seven had one vote each in the school council which met every week. Rules were made, complaints raised, and malefactors punished or arrangements made for reparation. Even at Summerhill, however, not all matters were settled by the council. Sleeping arrangements, food, payment of bills and the appointment of teachers were organized by Neill and his wife.[7] Clearly, weekly meetings and discussions take time, but if they are considered important time will be found, and if one result is that children accept the decisions that are made, then some of the time that would otherwise be spent on rule enforcement will be saved as well. One of the arguments against children being allowed to make important decisions for themselves is that they lack the capacity to look far ahead. Insofar as this is true it will result in decisions being made, changed and made again, but although is may be wearying for the adults involved it is part of the educative process. Rules will be made when the need for them is apparent,[8] and it may be necessary for each new generation of children to discover the need for themselves.

Beacon Rise, the school founded by Bertrand and Dora Russell, was also small enough for democratic decisions to be made through discussion involving all the pupils. Dora Russell said:

> This was a democracy in which people had to learn by experience and discussion how to live amicably with one another. To bring up a child

under a rigid system of authority, enforcing implicit obedience ... seemed to us a poor preparation for life in a democratic society. The likely result of such treatment would be either timid conformers or refractory rebels. But living day by day in discussion with those who were virtually your equals in age and attainments could lead you to acquire, both emotionally and rationally, the democratic qualities of mutual understanding and tolerance.[9]

The debate about the best size for a school is always with us, with claims for the advantages of large schools on the grounds of cost effectiveness and availability of specialist staff being argued against the family atmosphere and intimate knowledge of pupils which may be found in small schools. This is not the place to pursue these arguments. However, I would claim that small scale direct democracy is better suited to the needs of children than is representative democracy, both as a way of making day-to-day decisions which can be seen to be fair, and of introducing the concept of democracy in a clear way. Larger schools have other advantages, and in these schools ways must be sought to overcome the problems of size.[10]

The head of a state secondary school in New Zealand who had attempted to encourage democracy in his school claims that it is better to let the pupils elect *ad hoc* committees with clearly defined powers and responsibilities for certain specific purposes rather than to have a school council with no real power. He writes:

We have gone through swings and shifts and these I recognize as educational processes in themselves. Thus our seniors have voted out, in, out and in the prefect system; they have tried and rejected the School Council as such; they have veered from no uniform for 7th formers and glide time to uniform and strict hours[11]

If this sounds a bit chaotic, it should be remembered that this headteacher was not trying to find a correct decision on whether it is right to have either prefects or uniforms. He wanted the pupils to decide for themselves, and recognized that what suits one year group may not suit another, and that sometimes the only thing that makes one course of action better than another is that the people involved are happy with it. What is important in this instance is the educational value of debate and decision-making which must, like all other school work, be done afresh by each new class. Teachers may have to listen to arguments on the same subjects year after year and be helpful and sympathetic while arrangements are changed and then changed back again, but if they are convinced that it is important and educative for pupils to be involved in the making of decisions then they will do it. It will not be easy, but then teaching is not an easy job.

Democracy for the Staff

The first head of Countesthorpe College also wanted to involve the pupils in decision-making, but first he took the step that I consider crucial to the success of a democratic school: he involved the staff. Brian Simon explains that a decision was made:

> that the school was to be run by the staff as a whole, through discussion and joint decisions arrived at by consensus. The head would participate in the discussion but would carry out decisions so reached . . . This step . . was seen as a means of ensuring that each and every member of the school's staff could feel a genuine and equal responsibility for running the school, so that participation and involvement could be maximized. [12]

The participation of the staff was considered important in order that the school should continue to be innovative and flexible. So often a new head will initiate change, but then the school becomes static. As the impetus for change often comes from younger staff, who are usually newer and more junior, a democratic structure is necessary if they are to make their contribution. However, equally or even more important reasons for having a democratic staffroom as well as pupil representation are that it helps to ensure that the staff are united in their attempts to increase the democratic participation and the liberty of the pupils, and that it provides the children with an example of equals sharing responsibility, discussing, arguing, disagreeing and coming to a decision which binds them all.

Comparing various schools which have tried to increase children's liberty and democratic participation, I found that having a staff that is united and enthusiastic about the venture is of critical importance. Most free schools will attract some measure of antagonism from outside. Private free schools have sometimes to face the wrath of the neighbourhood and local press, but at least they should have the support of parents and teachers who have chosen the school, knowing its philosophy. State schools do not have this advantage and have to win local support, and any dissent among the staff about their aims makes this much more difficult. As John Watts, the second head of Countesthorpe College said:

> An authoritarian progressive will usually come unstuck when outside agencies can exploit the division he has created among his staff. When this happens the reform aimed for by the head is thwarted, the power passes out of the school even to the point of its closing down and, more to the point, the children suffer.[13]

Both Risinghill Comprehensive and William Tyndale Junior School, which were closed by their local education authorities, had heads who wanted to increase children's freedom and democratic participation but did not have the full support of all their staff, and who were accused in their turn of not supporting the staff.[14] Gretton and Jackson tell of a deep division amongst the staff at William Tyndale which was exploited by unsympathetic governors and parents.[15] Nearby John Milton School apparently managed to weather many of the same problems, largely because the head and the teachers were united in their aims. In addition the school secretary and dinner ladies, all of whom shared a staff room, were invited to staff meetings, and helped to feel part of the school. As these ancillary workers were mostly parents as well, they were on the side of the staff, and understood what they were trying to do and why.

At Risinghill, many of the staff felt that the head did not support them or understand their problems, and that he had imposed a system on them that they did not believe in or could not make work.[16] At Countesthorpe, on the other hand, the staff worked together with the head, and managed to survive the adverse publicity and criticism which seems to be inevitable in the first few years. John Watts said that in a participatory system such as they had at Countesthorpe the role of the head is different.

> Instead of experiencing the gratification of seeing my own will take on flesh . . I now feel I have made possible and participated in a form of school in which teachers and school students have been able to enjoy an increase in dignity which results from their sense of determining to a large extent the conditions under which they work and grow.[17]

The inevitable compromises that will come in such a school might dismay a head who was determined to extend children's liberty and democratic participation, and feared the conservatism of the staff. However, it is not only for prudential reasons that teachers and other school staff ought to be involved in the running of the school. If heads genuinely believe that it is right for pupils to be involved in the making of decisions that affect them in their place of work, then they cannot, with any consistency, deny this to the teachers and other staff who also work there, and who should provide an example of democratic cooperation. There will be disagreements amongst the staff, of course, and sometimes, as we would expect, the decisions that are made by the pupils will be unwise, but so will some of their spellings be wrong, some writing illegible and some ideas ill-expressed.[18] Children are at school to learn and so, if we want them to learn about democracy, we should not regard petitions, deputations etc. as a nuisance or 'trouble', but as signs that they are interested in participation. School is the place to improve, and teachers should welcome the first clumsy attempts at participation just as they welcome the first bright green circle that is meant to be a picture of Mum.

Problems of Democracy

An important difference, however, between exercises in books and exercises in democracy is that mistakes in the former do not affect anyone but the pupil who makes them: mistaken democratic decisions affect others. Any democracy should be concerned to prevent the tyranny of the majority and to protect the rights and welfare of minorities and dissenting individuals, but this is particularly important in schools as the pupils are still learning democratic attitudes.

Frank Musgrove voices this concern about the danger to pupils if teachers give up their right to determine acceptable conduct and allow children to be self-governing in this respect. He says 'When schoolmasters do not control schoolboys, schoolboys do — but usually more repressively'[19] and he cites the example of nineteenth century public schools when the boys' activities outside lessons were governed largely by their own rules, and bullying was rife. However the situation of which Musgrove writes was not one in which cooperation and democracy were fostered. The boys may have been self-governing, but they were not democratic, just as a country which achieves independence can be self-governing and still have a despotic government. Teachers must always be on guard to see that bullying does not flourish, but I see no reason to suppose, as Musgrove does, that this is more likely to happen when pupils share power, or to equate the despotic rule of a self-appointed group with democracy in schools. Indeed, democracy is usually taken to be some defence against tyranny, and no teacher who valued it would, like the 19th century head of Winchester cited by Musgrove, refuse 'to be informed of schoolboy bullying out of a sensitive regard for traditions of schoolboy autonomy.'[20] Neill says that the Summerhill General School Meeting often had to tackle the problem of bullying[21] but that this was a problem the children took very seriously. I do not accept all Neill's claims for his school, but the one that bullying was less common than in strict schools seems reasonable. If children have a relaxed relationship with their teachers which enables them to speak of their worries, and if teachers know their pupils in a wider context than that of the classroom, there will be less scope for bullies to operate, and possibly they will feel less urge to work off their own frustrations and inadequacies on those who are smaller or weaker.

I have already stressed that participatory democracy involves more than electing leaders and more even than voting on a particular issue. There must be discussion — talking and listening — so that everyone's point of view is aired and, it is to be hoped, understood and whenever possible accommodated. This is a feature of democracy in small organizations which should be particularly stressed in schools and drawn to pupils' attention in the more formal political education which they receive. It tends to be overlooked if we turn to Westminster for our model of democracy and think that the point of a debate is to muster as many like-minded voters as we can, or, at a slightly higher level, persuade others to think as we do and vote with us. This may be necessary in a parliament of representatives, elected to carry out a party programme, but when everyone is their own representative and no-one is let down by a change of mind or policy; then, it should be remembered that listening is as important as talking, and understanding the opposition is as important as defeating it. If this is the democratic style which characterizes democracy in school there will be fewer occasions when a minority is left unhappy about the decisions reached, and it is even less likely that there will be a permanent minority that is consistently overruled and excluded from power.

Disaffected minorities, though less likely to be found in a small community like a school than in the country as a whole, may still occur. Perhaps one group of pupils in an Animal Rights Group might want to stop meat being served for school dinners, while a group of Muslim children might want to have Halal meat provided. Perhaps neither group would be satisfied by the result of a vote, and the problem would be complicated by the presence of a majority of children who do not have strong feelings either way. 'One person one vote' is thought to epitomize democratic justice. However, sometimes justice seems to demand that we should distinguish between those who are very much affected by a decision and those who are less so, or between the small group with strong feelings and those in the rest of the community who do not really mind.[22]

Even if there were answers to these problems and I knew them, this would not be the place to reveal them. My purpose here is to show that the problems of democracy in school are very similar to the problems of democracy in any other organization. Is X a decision which should be taken by the whole community or the group most affected by it? Is Y a decision that is of no concern to the whole group, and should properly be made by an individual? Is Z a decision that the group is not competent to decide, and which should be taken by an expert? These questions arise in our society every day. We argue about the answers to them, and it is right that we should. Our freedom to do so is highly valued, and greater freedom to be more directly involved in such discussion would reduce the power that others have over the important decisions of our lives. If the presence of problems and difficulties in our democracy are not thought to provide an adequate reason for abandoning it in society as a whole, then their presence in schools is not an adequate reason for arguing that we should not have democracy there. We should be careful of demanding perfection in school democracy when we do not expect it in other democratic institutions. The presumption, in schools as elsewhere, should be in favour of direct democratic participation whenever possible, with the onus on those who believe it is not appropriate in particular circumstances to demonstrate why.

Simone Weil said that:

> The least evil society is that in which the general run of men are most often obliged to think while acting, have the most opportunities for exercising control over collective life as a whole, and enjoy the greatest amount of independence.[23]

I would agree, and claim that the same should be said about schools — with the additional requirement, of course, that they educate their pupils. Children will not be able to participate as fully in the running of their society as most adults would, but a sincere valuation of democracy will involve maximizing opportunities for them to practise democracy as well as to learn about it. It is to be hoped that they will learn that there are problems to be faced in any demo-cratic organization, but that these will not be solved by abdicating our responsibilities and leaving what should be joint decisions to leaders. By participating in the exercise of power they will not find freedom, if by that we mean the freedom to do what they wish and make all the decisions that affect them as if no-one else mattered. Sometimes their wishes will be overruled. However they will gain important freedoms, and, in having some control over the power that other people can exercise over them, will safeguard others.

Democracy is not freedom; it does not guarantee freedom; but if we value the freedoms it does offer, then we should allow our children to share them as soon as they are able, and should educate them to join with others in the run-ning of our society. They are part of that society: it should be organized to cater for their needs and also to enable them to participate in it as fully as they are able, sharing the responsibilities and benefits of membership, its obligations and its liberties.

Notes and References

1. For a strong argument against schools which attempt to exist as islands, ignoring the problems and needs of the wider society see Kozol *Free Schools* p. 30–5
2. Joseph Schumpeter, 'Two Concepts of Democracy' in Anthony Quinton, (ed) *Political Philosophy*
3. Ministry of Education, *Half Our Future: a Report of the Central Advisory Council for Education*
4. J. S. Mill, Essays on Politics and Culture p. 186
5. Frank Musgrove, *Patterns of Power and Authority in English Education* p. 86
6. Peter Scrimshaw, *Values and Authority in Schools* p.70ff
7. A. S. Neill, *Summerhill* p. 54ff
8. Ibid. At Summerhill, for example, the question of bedtimes is discussed at the beginning of each term.
9. Dora Russell, *The Tamarisk Tree. 2* p. 28
10. In Countesthorpe College, for example, the school was divided into teams.
11. J. Garfield Johnson, 'Changing Institutions from the Inside.' in John E. Watson, *Policies for Participation* p. 127
12. Brian Simon, in Watts (ed) *The Countesthorpe Experience* p. 21
13. John Watts, op. cit. p. 125
14. Gretton and Jackson *William Tyndale: Collapse of a School and a System?* p. 57–8
15. Ibid.

16. Leila Berg, *Risinghill: Death of a Comprehensive*
17. Watts, op. cit. p. 129
18. This point is stressed by Pat White, *Beyond Domination* p. 129 'Just as no-one would expect to walk into a school and find stacks of exercise books filled with flawless work, so no-one should expect to hear of schools which run like clockwork with pupils exercising the judgment of a Nehru or a Kissinger and demonstrating the attitudes of a Martin Luther King.'
19. Musgrove, op. cit. p. 81
20. Ibid.
21. Neill, op. cit. p. 56
22. For example, a major point of contention in the 1984 Miners' strike was whether there should have been a national strike ballot. On the one hand it was argued that the men whose local associations had voted against the strike should not then be called out without a national ballot. On the other hand, miners from peripheral coalfields argued that the future of their pits and jobs should not be decided by the vote of those miners from more secure areas. The question of who was affected by the decision, and who should take it was bitterly disputed.
23 Simone Weil, *Oppression and Liberty* p. 103

Bibliography

Articles

A.C.E. (Advisory Centre for Education) (1971) 'A charter of children's rights.' *Where* 56, pp. 105–9

ALLISON, Lincoln, (1981) 'Liberty: a correct and authoritarian account.' *Political Studies* 29 pp. 376–91

AUDI, Robert (1974) 'Moral responsibility, freedom and compulsion.' *American Philosophical Quarterly* 11 pp. 1–14

BALDWIN, Tom (1984) 'MacCullum and the two concepts of freedom.' *Ratio* 26 pp. 125–42

BENN, S. I. and WEINSTEIN W., (1971) 'Being free to act and being a free man.' *Mind* LXXX pp. 194–211

BEREITER, Carl (1972) 'Moral alternatives to education.' *Interchange* 3

BERLIN, Isaiah (1964) 'Hobbes, Locke and Professor Macpherson.' *The Political Quarterly* 35 pp. 444–68

BRIDGES, David (1984) 'Non-paternalistic arguments in support of parents' rights.' *Journal of Philosophy of Education* 18 pp. 5–62

CARTER, Rosemary (1977) 'Justifying paternalism' *Canadian Journal of Philosophy* VII p 133–45

COKER, Francis W. (1953) 'Some present-day critics of liberalism' *The American Political Science Review* 47 pp. 1–27

DAY, J. P. (1977) 'Threats, offers, law, opinion and liberty' *American Philosophical Quarterly* 14 pp. 257–71

EWING, A. C. (1941–2) 'The rights of the individual against the state' *Proceedings of the Aristotelian Society* XLIII pp. i–xxxiv

GOLDMAN, Alvin I. (1972) 'Toward a theory of social power' *Philosophical Studies* 23 pp. 221–68

GUTMAN, Amy (1980) 'Children, paternalism and education: a liberal argument.' *Philosophy and Public Affairs* 9 pp. 338–58

HALLIDAY, R. J. (1968) 'Some recent interpretations of John Stuart Mill' *Philosophy* XLIII p. 1–17

HART, H. L. A. (1955) 'Are there any natural rights?' *Philosophical Review* 64 pp. 175–91

HOBSON, Peter (1984) 'Some reflections on parents' rights in the upbringing of their children.' *Journal of Philosophy of Education* 18 pp. 63–74

HODGES, Jill, (1981) 'Children and parents: who chooses?' *Politics and power* 3 pp. 49–65

HODSON, John D. (1977) 'The principle of paternalism' *American Philosophy Quarterly* 14 pp. 61–9

KATZ, M. S. (1977) 'Compulsion and the discourse on compulsory school attendance.' *Educational Theory* 27 pp. 179–85

KLEINIG, John (1976) 'Mill, children and rights' *Educational Philosophy and Theory* 8 pp. 1–15

KLEINIG, John (1981) 'Compulsory schooling' *Journal of Philosophy of Education* 15 pp. 191–204

LLOYD, D. I. (1980) 'The rational curriculum: a critique' *Journal of Curriculum studies* 12 pp. 331–42

MACDONALD, Margaret (1946–7) 'Natural rights' *Aristotelian Society Proceedings* XLVII p. 225–50

MCLAUGHLIN, T. H. (1984) 'Parental rights and the religious upbringing of children.' *Journal of Philosophy of Education* 18 pp. 784

PARENT, W. A. (1974) 'Some recent work on the concept of liberty.' *American Philosophical Quarterly* 11 p. 149–66

PARENT, W. A. (1974) 'Freedom as the non-restriction of options' *Mind* LXXXIII pp. 432–4

REED, T. M. and P. JOHNSTONE (1980) 'Children's Liberation' *Philosophy* 55 pp. 263–6

ROSENAK, Julia (1982 'Should children be subject to paternalistic restrictions on their liberties?' *Journal of Philosophy of Education* 16 pp. 89–97

SCARRE, Geoffrey (1980) 'Children and paternalism' *Philosophy* 55 pp. 117–24

SCHRAG, Francis (1975) 'The child's status in the democratic State' *Political Theory* 3 pp. 441–57

SCHRAG, Francis (1977) 'The child in the moral order' *Philosophy* 52 pp. 167–77

SOBLE, Alan (1982) 'Paternalism, liberal theory and suicide' *Canadian Journal of Philosophy* 12 pp. 335–52

WARE, Alan (1981) 'The concept of manipulation: its relation to democracy and power.' *British Journal of Political Science* 11 pp. 163–81

WHITE, D. M. (1969) 'Negative liberty' *Ethics* 80 pp. 185–204

WHITE, John (1981) 'In defence of state-controlled curricula' *Journal of Philosophy of Education* 15 pp. 255–60

Books

AITKENHEAD, Lois (Ed) (1978) *Children's Rights — Extinction or Rebirth*. Glasgow: S.C.C.L. and Heatherbank Press.

ACKERMAN, N. W. *et al.* (1970) *Summerhill: For and Against* New York: Hart Publishing Inc.

BARRY, Brian (1973) *The Liberal Theory of Justice*. Oxford: Clarendon Press.

BANTOCK, G. H. (1952) *Freedom and Authority in Education*. London: Faber and Faber.

BAY, Christian (1958) *The Structure of Freedom*. Stanford, California: Stanford University Press.

BENN, S. I. and R. S. PETERS (1959) *Social Principles and the Democratic State*. London: George Allen and Unwin.

BENTHAM, Jeremy (1843) *Collected Works*. (Ed. Bowring) Edinburgh: William Tait.

BERG, Leila (1972) *Risinghill: Death of a Comprehensive*. Harmondsworth: Penguin.

BERGER, Nan (1974) *Rights: a Handbook for People Under Age*. Harmondsworth: Penguin.

BERLIN, Isaiah (1969) *Four Essays on Liberty*. Oxford: Oxford University Press.

BLOCKER, H. Gene and Elizabeth H. SMITH (Eds) (1980) *John Rawls' Theory of Social Justice: an Introduction*. Athens: Ohio University Press.

BOSANQUET, Bernard (1920) *The Philosophical Theory of the State*. London: Macmillan.

BOULDING, Elise (1979) *Children's Rights and the Wheel of Life*. New Brunswick, New Jersey: Transaction Books.

BRAYBROOKE, David (1968) *Three Tests for Democracy*. New York: Random House.

BRENNAN, Tom (1981) *Political Education and Democracy*. Cambridge: Cambridge University Press.

BRIDGES, D. and P. SCRIMSHAW (Eds) (1975) *Values and Authority in Schools*. London: Hodder and Stoughton.

BROWN, S. C. (Ed) (1975) *Philosophers Discuss Education*. London and Basingstoke: Macmillan.

CARY, Joyce (1963) *Power in Men*. Seattle: University of Washington Press.

CHAPMAN, John W. (1968) *Rousseau — Totalitarian or Liberal?* New York: A.M.S. Press Inc.

CRANSTON, Maurice (1967) *Freedom: a New Analysis*. London: Longmans, Green and Co Ltd.

CRICK, Bernard (1963) *Political Theory and Practice*. London: Penguin.

CRICK, Bernard and Alex PORTER (1978) *Political Education and Political Literacy*. London: Longman.

CROSS, Gillian (1984) *The Demon Headmaster*. Harmondsworth: Puffin Books, Penguin.

DANIELS, Norman (Ed) (1975) *Reading Rawls: Critical Studies of 'A Theory of Justice'*. Oxford: Basil Blackwell.

DEWEY, John (1913) *School and Society*. Chicago: University of Chicago Press.

DEWEY, John (1925) *Democracy and Education*. New York: The Macmillan Company.

DEWEY, John (1963) *Experience and Education*. New York: Collier-Macmillan.

DOWNIE, R. S. and Elizabeth TELFER (1969) *Respect for Persons*. London: George Allen and Unwin.

DOYLE, James, F. (Ed) (1973) *Educational Judgments*. London: Routledge and Kegan Paul.

DWORKIN, Ronald (1977) *Taking Rights Seriously*. London: Duckworth.

ELLIS, Terry and Brian HADDOW, Dorothy McCOLGAN and Jackie McWHIRTER (1976) *William Tyndale: the Teachers' Story*. London: Writers and Readers Publishing Cooperative.

ENTWISTLE, Harold (1971) *Political Education in a Democracy*. London: Routledge and Kegan Paul.

FEINBERG, Joel (1973) *Social Philosophy* Englewood Cliffs, New Jersey: Prentice Hall.

FLEW, Antony (1976) *Sociology, Equality and Education*. London and Basingstoke: Macmillan.

GIBBS, Benjamin (1976) *Freedom and Liberation*. London: Sussex University Press.

GOODMAN, Paul (1962) *Compulsory Mis-education and the Community of Scholars*. New York: Random House.

GOUGH, J. W. (1957) *The Social Contract: A Critical Study of its Development*. Oxford: Clarendon Press.

GRAHAM, Keith (Ed) (1982) *Contemporary Political Philosophy*. Cambridge: Cambridge University Press.

GRAUBARD, Allen (1974) *Free the Children*. New York: Random House Inc.

GREEN, T. H. (1901) *Lectures on the Principles of Political Obligation*. London: Longmans, Green & Co.

GREENSTEIN, Fred I. (1965) *Children and Politics*. New Haven and London: Yale University Press.

GRETTON, John and Mark JACKSON (1976) *William Tyndale: Collapse of a School — or a System?* London: George Allen & Unwin.

HAMPSHIRE, Stuart (Ed) (1978) *Public and Private Morality*. Cambridge: Cambridge University Press.

HART, H. L. A. (1982) *Law, Liberty and Morality*. Oxford: Oxford University Press.

HAUBRICK, Vernon F. and Michael W. APPLE, (Eds) (1975) *Schooling and the Rights of Children*. Berkeley, California: McCutchan Publishing Corporation.

HAYEK, F. A. (1960) *The Constitution of Liberty*. London: Routledge and Kegan Paul.

HAYEK, F. A. (1978) *New Studies in Philosophy, Politics, Economics and the History of Ideas*. London: Routledge and Kegan Paul.

HEATER, D. B. (Ed) (1969) *The Teaching of Politics*. London: Methuen.

HOBBES, Thomas (1968) *Leviathan*. (Ed. Macpherson) Harmondsworth: Penguin.

HOBBES, Thomas (1972) *Man and Citizen*. (Ed. Gert) New York: Doubleday & Co.

HOBHOUSE, L. T. (1975) *The Elements of Social Justice*. London: George Allen and Unwin Ltd.

HOLT, John (1971) *The Under-achieving School*. Harmondsworth: Penguin.

HOLT, John (1972) *Freedom and Beyond*. Harmondsworth: Penguin.

HOLT, John (1975) *Escape from Childhood*. Harmondsworth: Penguin.

HOLT, John (1977) *Instead of Education*. Harmondsworth: Penguin.

KLEINIG, John (1982) *Philosophical Issues in Education*. London: Croom Helm.

KOZOL, Jonathan (1979) *Free Schools*. Boston: Houghton Mifflin Company.

LANGEVELD, Willem, (1972) *Political Education for Teenagers*. Strasbourg: Council for Cultural Co-operation/Council of Europe.

LASLETT, Peter, W. G. RUNCIMAN and Quentin SKINNER (Eds) (1972) *Philosophy, Politics and Society: 4th series*. Oxford: Basil Blackwell.

LASLETT, Peter and James FISHKIN (Eds) (1979) *Philosophy, Politics and Society: 5th series*. Oxford: Basil Blackwell.

LIVELY, Jack (1975) *Democracy*. Oxford, Basil Blackwell.

LOCKE, John (1963) *Two Treatises of Government*. Cambridge: Cambridge University Press.

LUCAS, J. R. (1976) *Democracy and Participation*. Harmondsworth, Penguin.

LUKES, Steven (1964) *Power: a Radical View*. London: Macmillan.

MACPHERSON, C. B. (1962) *The Political Theory of Possessive Individualism: Hobbes to Locke*. Oxford: Oxford University Press.

MACPHERSON, C. B. (1973) *Democratic Theory*. Oxford: Clarendon Press.

MCNEILLY, F. S. (1968) *The Anatomy of Leviathan*. London: Macmillan.

MAGEE, John (1971) *Philosophical Analysis in Education*. New York: Harper and Row.

MILL, J. S. (1962) *Essays on Politics and Culture*. (Ed. Himmelfarb) New York: Doubleday.

MILL, J. S. (1984) *Utilitarianism, On Liberty and Considerations on Representative Government*. (Ed. Acton) London: Dent.

MILNE, A. J. M. (1968) *Freedom and Rights*. London: George Allen and Unwin.

MUSGROVE, Frank (1971) *Patterns of Power and Authority in English Education*. London: Methuen.

NEILL, A. S. (1971) *Summerhill*. Harmondsworth: Penguin.

NOONE, John B. (1981) *Rousseau's Social Contract: a Conceptual Analysis*. London: George Prior.

NOZICK, Robert (1974) *Anarchy, State and Utopia*. Oxford: Basil Blackwell.

O'NEILL, Onora and William RUDDICK (Eds) (1979) *Having Children: Philosophical and Legal Reflections on Parenthood*. New York: Oxford University Press.

PATEMAN, Carole (1970) *Participation and Democratic Theory*. Cambridge: Cambridge University Press.

PATEMAN, Carole (1979) *The Problem of Political Obligation*. Chichester: John Wiley and Sons.

PENNOCK, J. Roland and John W. CHAPMAN (Eds) (1972) *Coercion*. Chicago/New York: Aldine Atherton Inc.

PENNOCK, J. Roland (1972) *Democratic Political Theory.* Princetown, New Jersey: Princetown University Press.

PETERS, R. S. (Ed) (1973) *Education, Democracy and the Public Interest.* London: Oxford University Press.

PHILLIPS GRIFFITHS, A. (Ed)(1983) *Of Liberty.* Cambridge: Cambridge University Press.

PICKLES, Dorothy (1971) *Democracy.* London: Methuen.

PLATO (1965) *The Republic.* (Tr. H. D. P. Lee) Harmondsworth: Penguin.

QUINTON, Anthony (Ed) (1967)*Political Philosophy.* Oxford: Oxford University Press.

RAPHAEL, D. D. (Ed) (1967) *Political Theory and the Rights of Man.* London: Macmillan.

RAPHAEL, D. D. (1981) *Problems of Political Philosophy.* London: Macmillan.

RAWLS, John (1980) *A Theory of Justice.* Oxford: Oxford University Press.

REIMER, Everett (1975) *School is Dead.* Harmondsworth: Penguin.

RICKENBACKER, William F. (Ed) (1974) *The Twelve Year Sentence: Radical Views of Compulsory Schooling.* La Salle, Illinois: Open Court Publishing Co.

ROUSSEAU, J-J. (1968) *The Social Contract.* (Tr. Maurice Cranston) Harmondsworth: Penguin.

ROUSSEAU, J-J. (1969) *Emile.* (Tr. Barbara Foxley) London: J. M. Dent and Sons.

RUSSELL, Dora (1981) *The Tamarisk Tree. Volume 2: My School and the Years of War.* London: Virago.

RYAN, Alan (Ed) (1979) *The Idea of Freedom.* Oxford: Oxford University Press.

SANDEL, Michael J. (1982) *Liberalism and the Limits of Justice.* Cambridge: Cambridge University Press.

SARGENT, Lyman Tower (1978) *Contemporary Political Ideologies: a Comparative Analysis.* Homewood, Illinois: The Dorsey Press.

SCHOCHET Gordon J. (1971) *Life, Liberty and Property: Essays on Locke's Political Ideas.* Belmont, California: Wadsworth Publishing Co.

SCHOOL OF BARBIAN A (1970) *Letter to a Teacher.* Harmondsworth: Penguin.

SKIDELSKY, Robert (1969) *English Progressive Schools.* Harmondsworth: Penguin.

SNOOK, I. A. (Ed) (1972) *Concepts of Indoctrination.* London: Routledge and Kegan Paul.

SPINOZA, B. de (1854) *A Treatise on Politics.* (Tr. William Maccall) London: Holyoake.

STRIKE, Kenneth A. and Keiran EGAN (Eds) (1978) *Ethics and Educational Policy.* London: Routledge and Kegan Paul.

STRIKE, Kenneth (1982) *Liberty and Learning.* Oxford: Martin Robertson.

TAYLOR, Michael (1982) *Community, Anarchy and Liberty.* Cambridge: Cambridge University Press.

VARDIN, Patricia A. & Ilene N. BRODY (Eds) (1979) *Children's Rights: Contemporary Perspectives.* New York/London: Teachers' College Press.

VAUGHAN, Mark (Ed) (1972) *Rights of Children*. Nottingham: N.C.C.L. (Russell Press).

WALES, John N. (1962) *Schools of Democracy*. Michegan: Michegan State University Press.

WARRENDER, Howard (1957) *The Political Philosophy of Hobbes*. Oxford: Clarendon Press.

WATSON, John E. (Ed) (1977) *Policies for Participation*. Wellington, N. Z.: N. Z. Education Administration Society.

WATTS, John (Ed) (1977) *The Countesthorpe Experience*. London: George Allen and Unwin.

WEIL, Simone (1958) *Oppression and Liberty*. London: Routledge and Kegan Paul.

WHITE, John (1973) *Towards a Compulsory Curriculum*. London: Routledge and Kegan Paul.

WHITE, John (1983) *The Aims of Education Restated*. London: Routledge and Kegan Paul.

WHITE, Patricia (1983) *Beyond Domination*. London: Routledge and Kegan Paul.

WILLIAMS, Bernard and Alan MONTEFIORE (Eds) (1966) *British Analytical Philosophy*. London: Routledge and Kegan Paul.

WOLFF, Robert Paul (1968) *The Poverty of Liberalism*. Boston: Beacon Press.

WOLFF, Robert Paul (1970) *In Defense of Anarchism*. New York: Harper and Row.

WOLFF, Robert Paul (1977) *Understanding Rawls: a Reconstruction and Critique of "A Theory of Justice"*. Princetown, New Jersey: Princetown University Press.

WOODHOUSE, A. S. P. (Ed) (1938) *Puritanism and Liberty*. London: J. M. Dent and Sons Ltd.

WRINGE, C. A. (1981) *Children's Rights*. London: Routledge and Kegan Paul.

WRINGE, Colin (1984) *Democracy, Schooling and Political Education*. London: George Allen and Unwin.

Index

action(s) 3–4
    freedom of 27, 84, 86, 108, 116
    and paternalism 60–1, 68, 70–1, 75
    and rights 36, 37–8
ancillary workers 129
authority
    absolute 47
    and contracts 12–13, 19–20
    democratic 21
    and education 116, 126–7, 129
    freedom and 12, 105
    and rights 47, 79
autonomy
    of choice 70, 72, 86
    of individual 22, 72, 81
        in democracy 28
        in education 86, 88, 89, 98, 110, 131
    moral 28–9, 47

Baker, R. P. 92, 100
Beacon Rise School 126–7
Benn, S. I. and Peters, R. S. 39
Berlin, I. 2–4, 6–7
brainwashing 8, 65–6
bullying 5, 130–1
Burt, R. A. 45–6

children
    freedom of 1, 50, 53, 106, 107, 128
    as persons 48–9, 51
    see also choice; compulsory
        education; freedom, academic; freedom,
        increasing; restriction(s); rights
Children's Rights, UN Charter of 42
Children's Rights movement 45, 49

choice, freedom of 6, 84
    for children, 1, 53–4, 124
        in education 86–92, 99–101
        in schools 106–7, 109–10, 112–16
    in democracy 21–2, 24–5, 27–8, 125–6
    and paternalism 61, 63, 66, 67–70
    restriction of 7, 9
    and rights 34, 53–4, 57–8
citizens 82, 105, 115
    in democracy 21, 24–5, 29, 119, 120–1, 124
    and rights 33, 35–6, 56–7
civil liberty 3
coercion
    in democracy 26
    in education 83–4, 87, 91, 110
    and freedom 3, 5, 34, 84
    intentional 7, 9
    and paternalism 61–7, 69, 71–2, 74, 77, 80–1
    and rights 38, 45–6, 50, 52–4
    and uniformity 89
    unintentional 6, 9
compulsory education 82–103, 119
    compensation for 99–100
    curriculum 86–9
    and freedom 90–3
    incompatible with education 93–5
    and protection 97–9
    and restriction of freedom 83–6
consent
    and paternalism 65–6, 68, 70, 71–2, 74, 81
    to restrictions 12–20, 21, 124
        contracts 12–17
        to improve freedom 15–16
        obligations 18–20
    retrospective 65–6, 69